Improve Your Primary School Through Drama

Rachel Dickinson,
Jonothan Neelands
and
Shenton Primary School

9

 David Fulton Publishers

David Fulton Publishers Ltd
The Chiswick Centre, 414 Chiswick High Road, London W4 5TF

www.fultonpublishers.co.uk

First published in Great Britain in 2006 by David Fulton Publishers.

10 9 8 7 6 5 4 3 2 1

Note: The right of the individual contributors to be identified as the authors of their work has been asserted by them in accordance with the Copyright, Designs and Patents Act 1988.

British Library Cataloguing in Publication Data
A catalogue record for this book is available from the British Library.

David Fulton Publishers is a division of ITV plc.

ISBN 1 84312 306 1

Typeset by RefineCatch Ltd, Suffolk
Printed and bound in Great Britain

Contents

Acknowledgements   iv

Contributors   iv

Introduction   v

1 Improving your primary school through drama   1

2 From national policy to local practice   16

3 Getting ready for drama   35

4 Beginning with story   58

5 Acting to learn   91

6 Making a common unity: inclusion through differentiation   117

7 Measuring success   142

Appendix: NCSL performance indicators   158

References   166

Index   167

Acknowledgements

This book is dedicated to the staff, pupils, families and wider community of Shenton Primary School, Leicester, who showed the way. We also want to thank Tony Goode, Chris Davies, and Joe Winston for professional advice, support and critical friendship during this project. Thanks to Maggie and Steve for believing in us, and to Kate and Ben for believing in a better world. We also want to give respect to Dorothy Heathcote and David Booth whose time is always coming and whose ideas have influenced this book.

Contributors

This book includes the voices and journal writing of these teachers and other staff members from Shenton Primary School:

Meera Bulsara	Drama Co-ordinator and Foundation Years class teacher
Dionne Christian	Year 6 class teacher
Helen Gosling	Year 4 class teacher
Alan Greatrix	Year 1 class teacher
Gary Hawthorne	Behaviour mentor
Samina Khan	Learning Support Assistant Year 2
Smita Lad	Literacy Co-ordinator and Year 2 class teacher
Hajra Mullah	Deputy Head Teacher
Rachel Roberts	Key Stage 2 Manager and Year 6 class teacher
Maggie Welton	Head Teacher

Introduction

Who is this book for?

This book is about using drama as a school improvement strategy in primary schools. It gives guidance and advice on teaching drama from the foundation years to the end of Key Stage 2. There is a particular emphasis on the pedagogy of drama – ie on teaching and learning through drama. It does not give specific guidance on other important aspects of drama in schools, such as assemblies or school performances. The focus is on using drama to improve the quality of learning and the quality of life in a school, rather than on defining drama as a subject in its own right. We look at the 'value added' by regular classroom uses of drama.

The book will be particularly useful to the following people:

○ **Head teachers and those with a management responsibility** will use it to develop their own uses of drama as part of a school improvement strategy. They will also find national policy frameworks both for drama and for effective teaching and learning in the primary years. Throughout the book we offer evidence of drama's effectiveness as a school improvement strategy and give suggestions for curriculum and professional development activities.
○ **Experienced class teachers** will find specific advice on teaching drama as a subject and as a cross-curricular resource, ideas for lessons, and guidance on assessment and differentiation. They will also be encouraged by the experiences of real teachers working in challenging circumstances.
○ **Newly qualified teachers and student teachers** will use this as a guide to preparing to teach drama and the skills, concepts and understandings needed to make drama an effective way of teaching creatively. The focus on behaviour management and teaching strategies may be particularly useful for those entering urban primary schools.
○ **Learning support assistants (LSAs) and other classroom staff and helpers** will find the book helpful as they prepare to support drama in the classroom and become actively involved and professionally valued in drama sessions. It also offers clear explanations of why drama is important to children, as well as advice about some of the challenges they might face.

Structure of the book and synopsis of chapters

This book is written in seven chapters. Each of these addresses different aspects of drama policy and practice. There is a mix of advice and guidance, together with examples based in best practice and national guidance on drama in the primary years. This synopsis is a useful guide to what to expect in each chapter for ease of reference. The Reference list at the back of the book gives details of the key policy documents and other publications referred to, but a full list of resources for putting together a drama policy for your own school can be found on the publisher's website (www.fultonpublishers.co.uk).

1 Improving your primary school through drama

This chapter, with a title that echoes that of the book, sets out the reasons for our belief that drama can improve your primary school. Thus it provides a foundation for the rest of the book. We explain what we mean by improvement, the importance of feeling the school is 'your' school, and the significance of the primary years in laying the foundations for each child's growth as a healthy and positive individual. Finally, we define what we mean by drama and how it can impact on the whole curriculum – including the social, spiritual and emotional needs of the children.

2 From national policy to local practice

This chapter shows what the policy developed for Shenton Primary School owes to the national policy documents and other guidance on drama. Lessons can be drawn from this as to how these national guidelines can be adapted for any other individual school. We also consider other relevant guidance on pedagogy of creative teaching and learning and look at ways in which creative teaching in drama can lead to more creative teaching across the curriculum.

3 Getting ready for drama

This chapter begins with an overview of the key issues to consider when you are preparing for the challenges of drama work. It then looks at contracting ground rules for drama work based on negotiation and dialogue with the class. Key strategies for managing behaviour and creating a positive learning environment are described. This section also contains a checklist for analysing and reflecting on problems that might emerge. At the end of the chapter there is a sample lesson structure that we use to highlight and respond to potential problems that might emerge during the drama work.

4 Beginning with story

We go on to look in detail at how stories can be used as a starting point for drama work. We discuss the 'learning power of story' in the primary years and how traditional stories can be used as a comfortable starting point for drama. There is advice on selecting stories and selecting different ways of starting a story drama based on needs identification. In the final section we consider how a story can be used and accessed at different stages in the primary years and how to use story as a means of making connections across the curriculum

5 Acting to learn

Two key drama strategies – 'Teacher-in-Role' and 'Mantle of the Expert' – are presented in this chapter, along with advice and examples for each way of working. The final section of the chapter identifies other key drama techniques. An example of a Year 6 lesson based on *King Lear* demonstrates how these techniques can be used to develop and deepen role play.

6 Making a common unity: inclusion through differentiation

In this chapter we consider what 'differentiation' means in drama, and what its purposes are. We stress the need for differentiation as a strategy for social and cultural inclusion, as much as for raising standards of individual achievement in the academic curriculum. Strategies are presented for including pupils with English as an additional language (EAL), with special educational needs (SEN) and those identified as gifted and talented (G&T). We give an example of how differentiation for these groups might be applied in a scheme of work based on a picture story book.

7 Measuring success

The assessment process we used for drama at Shenton Primary is described as an example for other schools. A model for progression from Nursery to Year 6, both in artistic learning about drama and the social learning required by drama, is put forward. The 'Steps to Success in Drama' are given as an example of a local assessment framework that is benchmarked against national standards.

We go on to describe the talk-related 'assessment for learning strategies' used by learners and teachers in drama. We look at how these, together with choices of teaching style, bring the local 'Steps to Success' and 'Model of Progression' alive. Finally, we offer a framework for evaluating the contribution that drama makes to a school improvement programme by benchmarking evidence with nationally agreed standards of excellence.

At the end of the book, you can find an Appendix showing 'Performance indicators proposed by the NCSL' with evidence from Shenton's drama programme to match. There is also a list of key references and resources. Additional support material and resources can be found on the publisher's website (www.fultonpublishers.co.uk).

Related titles of interest

Drama and English at the Heart of the Curriculum: Primary and Middle Years, by Joe Winston. ISBN 1 84312 059 3

Beginning Drama 4–11, 2nd edition, by Joe Winston and Miles Tandy. ISBN 1 85346 702 2

Beginning Drama 11–14, 2nd edition, by Jonothan Neelands. ISBN 1 84312 086 0

Starting Drama Teaching, 2nd edition, by Mike Fleming. ISBN 1 85346 788 X

Drama Lessons for Five to Eleven-year-olds, by Judith Ackroyd and Jo Boulton. ISBN 1 85346 739 1

Speaking, Listening and Drama, by Andy Kempe and Jan Holroyd. ISBN 1 84312 041 0

Planning Creative Literacy Lessons, edited by Andrew Lambirth. ISBN 184312 280 4

Improving your primary school through drama

This chapter:

o puts forward the case for drama as a means of improving your primary school;
o explores the meaning of 'improvement';
o emphasises the importance of a sense of 'ownership' of your school;
o considers the influence of the primary years in laying the foundations for each child's growth as a healthy and positive individual;
o defines what we mean by 'drama' and how it can impact on the whole curriculum, including the social, spiritual and emotional needs of the children.

Local context

First of all, we should put our claim in context. This book is the result of three years of work with the staff and children of Shenton Primary School in Leicester, who established drama as a vital school resource enjoyed by all pupils, staff and parents. This work was done during a particularly challenging period for this urban school with a predominantly Muslim intake from many different countries. The school has 450 pupils on roll. Ninety-seven per cent of the pupils have English as an additional language (EAL) and 18 per cent of pupils have been identified as having special educational needs (SEN). There is a nursery attached to the school.

As the work developed we were all aware that drama was beginning to have positive effects on the life of the school as a learning and teaching community as well as improving the quality of classroom learning for pupils. The advantages we saw are presented in the three bulleted lists below.

Advantages for pupils

o Drama has successfully provided social learning in mixed ability settings for all pupils including those with English as an additional language (EAL), special educational needs (SEN) and those who are gifted and/or talented (G&T).

o Drama has increased empathy and tolerance of 'difference'.

o Acting and performing in front of others has increased confidence and improved communication and self-presentation skills.

o The focus on differentiation and behaviour management in drama has helped pupils to feel that their cultural, emotional and personal needs are considered in planning and teaching.

o Learning to work positively together in the social learning context of drama has affected group and class work across the curriculum.

o Improvements in behaviour and pupil relationships means more time on tasks across the curriculum.

o The positive 'can do' climate in drama has encouraged children to find their voices and use them without fear of censure or ridicule.

o Pupils are more willing to take risks in terms of cross-gender and cross-cultural learning and working together; they are more open to influences beyond their home and faith cultures.

Advantages for teachers and other staff

o Teachers feel a real sense of ownership because the drama initiative is in their control.

o The drama initiative has involved staff in openly taking risks together and the collegial approach has increased professional respect among teachers and others.

o Teachers have felt confident enough to discuss problems and concerns as well as successes.

o Teachers are more willing and likely to take informed risks in other areas of teaching and learning.

o Teachers have enjoyed 'exploring' stories and situations with their pupils in drama and learning from the pupils' contributions and ideas.

o Teachers are supported and encouraged at every level to take informed risks and have more confidence in this as a result of their successes in drama.

o Increased confidence and skill in using questioning and learning through discovery allows teachers to give greater responsibility to pupils for the direction of their learning.

Advantages for parents and the community

o Because parents have discussed drama with their children and been involved in workshops, they feel involved in the aims and objectives of the programme.

o Parents report that pupils talk enthusiastically about their drama work at home.

o Mulannas and other community leaders have been actively involved in shaping and supporting the drama programme.
o Governors have taken an active role in the strategy and now understand more about creative approaches to teaching and learning.
o Pupils invite their parents into school to share in their achievements in drama.

Our claims for the power of drama are based on the real experiences of teachers, children and their communities. We are confident that the ideas, examples and schemes of work offered in this book will be effective, because they are all based on what actually happens in Shenton. An ordinary school just like yours; an extraordinary school just like yours.

Improving the quality of learning and the quality of life

So what exactly do we mean by 'improvement'? School improvement often refers either to the restructuring of the school's management and other systems to make teaching and learning more efficient and effective, or to the introduction of specific strategies for improving pupils' success in the basics of literacy and numeracy in particular. Often, the pressure to 'improve' and the means of improvement are the result of external influences on the school from local or national inspectors and from national programmes and strategies.

Our approach is different. We believe that the focus of school improvement should be on developing the quality of teaching and learning, and the quality of life, for everyone involved in the community of the school. We believe that this is most likely to happen when teachers work together to reflect and act on the needs of their pupils, and their own desire to offer their pupils the best quality education in an inclusive curriculum that provides for the full range of human ability and abilities. In our experience, when teachers are inspired and supported to develop the classroom teaching and interpersonal skills needed for effective drama, they also transform the quality of life in the school. As we will see, there is a transferable pedagogy of drama which can also benefit teaching and learning in other subjects. We will show that drama can simultaneously address and enrich both the academic curriculum and the broader curriculum of pupils' social, emotional and spiritual needs.

For us then, introducing drama into a school will focus teachers in developing a wider range of skills and techniques. In order to teach drama effectively, teachers need some knowledge and understanding of drama and how it works, but they also need to work out:

o how to organise group work effectively;
o how to lead discussion;

o how to use questioning skills;
o how to encourage boys and girls to work together;
o how to negotiate behaviour in open spaces like the school hall;
o how to expect and allow pupils to take responsibility for their own learning and assessment;
o how to take informed risks;
o how to integrate subjects meaningfully;
o how to find a broader range of assessment tools than the traditional test.

In developing their skills in response to these challenges, teachers are also given the confidence to use a wider range of teaching and learning styles in their classrooms and to put a greater emphasis on the quality of relationships with pupils and among pupils.

This holistic approach to school improvement through drama is reflected in our core objectives for drama:

1 to provide meaningful and relevant contexts for our pupils to learn in;
2 to encourage our pupils to become actively involved in their learning;
3 to provide opportunities for our pupils to express themselves in all aspects of their learning;
4 to build confidence and raise self-esteem;
5 to create opportunities for our pupils to work positively with difference.

Staff agreed these objectives after an extensive analysis of the needs of the pupils. None of them relate directly to drama as a discrete subject – they are all focused on using drama as a response to the broader academic and pastoral needs of the pupils.

The following example gives us a glimpse of drama in practice and begins to explain how these broad objectives can impact on the quality of 'life' in the classroom.

The Tudors at sea

Azmat joined Year 4 a few weeks into the spring term. He was a new arrival from India and although he had relatives in the school, Azmat himself had extremely limited spoken and written English. At this time we were studying the lives of the Tudor sailors on board ship during the reign of Elizabeth I as part of our History curriculum. To support the children's understanding of the sailor's activities, living conditions and feelings, we were using drama as a tool to create empathy, develop historical language and to develop experience and ability to work in role.

In class the children had explored Tudor sailors using information books, pictures and simple artefacts. They had listened to readings of accounts by Tudor sailors and been encouraged to gather further information for homework. Azmat was able to look at the pictures in the classroom and handle the artefacts but was limited in his level of understanding, even when supported by a Gujarati speaker, as the whole concept was completely new for him.

We were at the stage in our drama activities where the children were creating still images in groups to suggest the different activities that happened on board ship. Azmat was placed into a group and was given some initial instructions by our learning support assistant (LSA) in his mother tongue. Despite being rather shy and no doubt overwhelmed by the activity, Azmat was moulded into the character of a Tudor sailor by the other children. Together they gave him dual language instructions and showed how to stand and hold his image. A fantastic example of teamwork! His facial expression took on a serious and determined look as he stood strong and proud, saluting the captain of the ship. His whole body image screamed out in the universal language of gesture and for the first time since his arrival Azmat was communicating with every single person in the room without the need to struggle to say a single word!

In this example, Helen, the class teacher, is working with multiple learning objectives. She is developing empathy across cultures and time, between the life worlds of migrant children like Azmat and the distant experiences of Elizabethan sailors. She is also introducing and using history-specific language and knowledge through physical and emotional engagement in drama situations that encourage pupils to think and feel authentically, imagining themselves into the shoes of Elizabethan sailors. She is also developing the pupils' drama skills in creating, developing and maintaining the roles of the sailors and captain. But at the heart of this example is the image of Azmat finding and contributing at last to his new community of classmates. He finds a voice where there was silence, supported and encouraged by his classmates. He finds that through drama, he can imagine himself differently and in so doing, bridge the gulf between his own story, culture and heritage and the strangeness of his new school and his new 'National Curriculum'.

The example shows that drama has provided a meaningful and relevant context for studying history; it has actively involved all the pupils, including Azmat; it has allowed for creative expression at an emotional level and it has built Azmat's confidence and self-esteem in the class. It has also blurred the differences between cultures both at the level of the historical content and also at the level of the 'difference' between Azmat and his classmates. (See Resource 5: *Tudors at Sea*; on the publisher's website, www.fultonpublishers.co.uk)

We don't make any promises about raising standards in terms of levels of achievement in specific subjects. Like Azmat's class teacher we are concerned with the quality of life and learning in the school in terms that may often be immeasurable by standard tests. We believe that this incident will have effects beyond the drama. Azmat has had a positive experience that he will remember and want to share with his family and friends. They will be reassured that Azmat is settling in to his new school, that he has been accepted by his classmates and is beginning to contribute to classwork despite his shaky grasp of English. The quality of life in and out of school will be improved for all pupils if the class can learn from this event to be as supportive of each other in the classroom, playgrounds and streets in which they live together as they were in the drama. In taking responsibility both for their own learning and in giving Azmat the tools and support he needed to be fully involved in the drama, the class have modelled the qualities of respect, tolerance and social responsibility which are essential to the success of our schools, and of urban schools in particular.

Your school and professional community

So far we have used examples from one school – a school like yours, but also different from yours. We are not suggesting that the Shenton example should be used as a template for all schools. The whole point is that teachers at Shenton shaped their drama curriculum in response to their own local context just as you must. They did not begin with government prescriptions or national initiatives; they did not borrow from anonymously produced policy documents or schemes of work and assessment, which ignore the particularities of each and every school. They began with their own analysis of the children, teachers, other staff and families who make up the special and unique community. They identified the particular contribution that they wanted drama to make. They delighted in being able to shape the school rather than being shaped by the limits of the National Curriculum and the National Literacy and Numeracy Strategies.

It is important to make time for staff to come together as a learning community to reflect on what makes their school special; what works and doesn't work for their pupils; what the community expects from the school and how best to respond to these expectations; how drama can help to maximise the strengths of pupils and staff and minimise the problems and obstacles to learning which are part of the reality of every school. Unless staff are willing to invest time at the beginning in developing and taking ownership of a drama initiative that is tailored to the special character of the school, it is unlikely that drama will take root and begin to produce examples like our Azmat story.

Making drama happen – a management strategy

Maggie, the headteacher, offers these words of advice to other school managers who see the potential of drama in a school improvement programme:

o Generate a personal vision for drama within the school and ensure that all key staff, governors and the Standards Inspector can share in that vision.
o Ensure drama is within the school improvement plan with clear action plans for the next three years that include learning and teaching, working with parents in the community, and equal opportunities.

o Employ a specialist teacher/facilitator to help and ensure that staff entitlement to training provision is realised.
o Create the position of drama co-ordinator; someone who will both organise and champion drama across the life of the school.
o Ensure that the staff have clear learning objectives for drama embedded within schemes of work.
o As a first step, opportunity for full and frank discussion needs to be made a priority to ensure that teachers can express their concerns.
o The specialist training provider or co-ordinator needs to model good practice with individual teachers so that they can see the potential of drama with their own classes.
o Teachers need time to be made available to reflect on and evaluate their own and others' drama work. It is only then that the value of teaching drama can be appreciated and shared.

This advice stresses the importance of embedding drama in the school improvement plan so that it remains at the centre of school policy implementation. It acknowledges the need for enthusiastic leadership, a collegial approach to developing drama and the important role of the drama co-ordinator in both championing and co-ordinating the implementation of drama. The need for personalised training and expert help in modelling good practice so that individual teachers can be confident that drama will work for their class is also central to the 'vision'. Making time during staff meetings and other staff development events for teachers to share experiences, plan together and voice any concerns is also vital to sustaining staff morale and interest in developing drama in their classrooms.

Making time is of course difficult. We would argue that drama is a good investment of time, in terms of the academic curriculum, because it combines artistic learning, cross-curricular connections and significant personal and social learning. In the same way, making time for staff to discuss and plan drama together will pay dividends in terms of mutual respect, the pooling of professional skills and encouraging a shared responsibility for improving the school. Allan, the ICT co-ordinator, captures this spirit well:

> What we have done in department meetings is to actually plan drama sessions together and to plan cross-curriculum links with drama sessions – so that all the Key Stage 1 team members gave support to each other. Then we have said, right, we are going to go away and try it and then come back and feed back, and talk about any potential or share good practice. I think that way you have a support network for people who aren't so confident, and actually an encouragement to try it because they know next week they are going to have to be asked about it.

Of course, the examples in this book come from a school in which the headteacher and governors agree to focus valuable resources on drama. Time is earmarked. Funding is secured to 'buy in' expert help. Other priorities are either given less 'value' or tackled through the drama programme. Drama is the main priority in the school, but other priorities as diverse as raising standards in literacy and improving behaviour in the playground are not ignored; they are addressed through the drama initiative. How can drama help us to improve literacy? How can we use drama to tackle anti-social behaviours? How can we shape our teaching to the particular needs of our pupils?

With a central place in the school improvement plan, drama can be harnessed for a variety of purposes related to the whole curriculum, including both academic and pastoral priorities. Vision, example and commitment can make drama happen, not just as a rare 'treat' at the margins of the curriculum, but as a central resource for improving the life of a school.

Meera, the drama co-ordinator, talks about her role and considers the effect drama is having on her own professional enthusiasm and that of other staff.

> Being the drama co-ordinator has enabled me to view teaching and learning from a different perspective. I now feel it is OK to take more risks and to teach in more unconventional ways. Drama has definitely put the fun and enthusiasm back into my own teaching. It is great to see teachers and children being more creative and seeing how powerful drama lessons can be on the development of the child as a whole.
>
> Drama is a great forum to get to know your class. Even though it is structured, there is so much scope for fun. It is lovely to have an atmosphere for relaxing and enjoying being and working with your class.
>
> As the drama co-ordinator I feel it is my responsibility to provide the support and opportunities for staff to be able to take more risks in their classrooms and within their teaching. I feel our school is in the midst of a creative journey and in my role I aim for all staff to share their new experiences.

Meera reminds us that at the heart of Shenton's plan to improve the quality of life and learning through drama lies the desire for a child-centred rather than National Curriculum- or external authority-centred approach. This means that staff began with an analysis of the range of teaching styles already used in the school and their impact on the children. The teachers were their own experts – sifting through their intimate knowledge of the children and what works for them. They were not responding to the demand to implement an externally imposed agenda shaped by 'experts' who had no real knowledge of these children, these teachers.

What can drama do?

What follows is the analysis made of teaching and learning styles based on the staff's collective wisdom and experience of how best to optimise learning for their pupils. This analysis might well reflect your own experiences of teaching your children in your school; it might also be quite a different picture from yours. It is offered here as an encouragement to begin from your own expert understandings of what works best for you and your children in your school.

This analysis is not specifically related to drama, it is an overarching view of pedagogy in practice in a school. Rather than being introduced as a new 'subject' or as a part of literacy, drama was introduced as a means of maximising the positives in the analysis and as a means of addressing some of the challenges. In this way drama was seen, for instance, as a means of providing interactive learning environments which were safe and fun for pupils, while also giving staff and pupils a means of meeting the challenges of working in large spaces and building self-esteem.

We see improvement as a positive process of identifying and developing the strengths of the staff and pupils. It is a 'self-realisation' project which encourages staff and pupils to make the most of what they have and can do together. The initial phase of introducing drama as a school improvement strategy is about identifying how drama can be used to improve the general quality of teaching and learning in a school and how it can be used to overcome some of the obstacles to learning. In this sense school improvement is the project, and drama is the means for making it happen.

Table 1.1 What do we know about how our pupils learn?

In what learning contexts do our pupils learn most effectively?	To what do they respond positively?
Meaningful contexts	Being actively involved
Group and pair work	Practical environments
Where there is co-operation and support from others	Multi-sensory opportunities
	Rewards
In an interactive learning environment	Praise
	Positive role models in teacher attitude
When learning is safe and fun	Working with responsibility
To what do they respond negatively?	**What do they find most challenging?**
	Working co-operatively
Being too directed	Sharing
When work does not relate to their own experiences	Access to English language
	Open spaces
Worksheets	Change
Work not given appropriate content/ context or related to their own experiences	

(continued)

Table 1.1   Continued

What motivates them?	What difficulties do they regularly experience in the classroom?
Time limits	
Positive praise	Asking questions
Seeing progress	Under-developed listening skills
Their achievements	Conflict with peers
Differentiated activities	Inability to mediate problems
Challenge	Managing themselves in open spaces
What triggers inappropriate behaviour?	**What are some of the barriers to their learning?**
Activities set at an inappropriate level	Tiredness
Frustration	Parents' limited use of English/literacy difficulties
Inability to communicate feelings	
Negative attention-seeking	Low self-esteem
	Low expectations

Drama offers a particularly appropriate opportunity for focusing on teaching and learning styles that will maximise the positives in this analysis. In order to do drama, a class and their teacher need to work together to create a 'meaningful' situation or context to work in; as villagers facing some environmental threat for instance. This context is built 'interactively' through group and pair work, which in turn requires support and co-operation. There has to be a context for learning in drama, there has to be a collective effort to make it work.

Drama also provides the space to work with the more negative features of the analysis. Creating a dramatic context requires pupils and their teacher to ask questions about the what, where, when, who and why of the drama. The class have to learn to control themselves physically in the open space used for drama. They have to develop the negotiating skills to respond together, as villagers, to a 'real' problem in the drama such as the effects of drought on their farms. Our argument is that through developing the skills necessary for effective drama work, pupils and teachers are also developing transferable skills that can improve the effectiveness of teaching and learning across the curriculum.

Primary school – a foundation for life

Your primary school is where children in your community get their start in life. It is a child's *primary* school, their first school; the school which will shape the rest of their school years and create a lasting impression on a child's sense of who they are and who they might become in the world. Of course, it is essential that this start should include developing the skills of literacy and numeracy, which are necessary for a fulfilling life in the future. And drama will have an important role in the development of literacy in particular, as we will see in later chapters. However, primary schools also have a responsibility for shaping the personal and social identities of children – they will have a significant influence upon the way children see themselves, others, and the world that they are growing into.

In this sense, the primary years of schooling are also about giving children the values, qualities, moral responsibilities, aspirations and dreams which will guide them toward adulthood. Primary schooling is not just about providing a foundation of skills and knowledge in the National Curriculum subjects in preparation for examination success in later years. It is also about modelling and shaping the healthy and successful citizens of the future. In order to do this the school needs to mirror the ideals and practices of a democratic, pluralist and diverse society.

In urban schools like Shenton, children are gathered from many different home and faith communities into the single community of the school. This school community must show children how to live together in a harmony based on respect, tolerance and an active involvement in ensuring that rights and responsibilities are upheld. It must be a community that listens and responds to individual needs while stressing the importance of working and living together in a shared world.

Learning to work together in drama was a great challenge, for staff and pupils alike. Children struggled to sit still, listen to each other, co-operate and take responsibility for creating rather than destroying work and to put the interests of the group before their own often selfish concerns. Just as democracy requires the willing acceptance of a social contract governing the behaviours, rights and responsibilities of citizens, so too does drama require agreements to be made by the whole class and the teacher so as to prevent the anti-social behaviours which get in the way of children being able to work positively together in the drama.

The processes of contracting, which every class went through in order to address the poor behaviour and lack of personal responsibility that characterised the early days, has had a positive effect on the school as a community in a much broader sense. Listen to this class teacher's example:

When negotiating the rules for our drama sessions I wanted the children to have as much ownership as possible over them and to support the contract by taking responsibility for their own learning. The rules would act as an agreement between myself, the class and each other, which we would enter into every time we came to work in the drama space.

Initially when the children were asked to suggest rules for their drama activities they were able to think of the basic rules associated with speaking and listening, such as raising your hand before you speak and listening to the teacher. With prompting and questioning, their ideas developed and I felt able to introduce the terms 'compromise' and 'negotiate'. We also established rules for how we would move in the space and value everyone as equal.

Through discussion and drama practice these rules have gradually become embedded in the children and the impact outside of the classroom has been immense. These rules can be applied easily to any area of the curriculum to address issues of equality, acceptance and independence, and because the children themselves have devised the rules they feel all the more empowered to use and apply them.

Drama and society

There are many examples of the role that drama has traditionally played in the formation of democratic societies, particularly urban societies. Think, for instance, of the role of drama in the lives of the fifth-century BC Athenians, or in late sixteenth-century and early seventeenth-century London. Historically, drama has offered people a 'mirror' for seeing themselves and how they behave. It has also offered a social means of questioning the world and articulating proposals for changing the world.

The primary school is a community and drama can play an important role in this community through performances, which bring the school community and the broader communities together to celebrate the achievements of the pupils. Children's performances can also make us all think about who we are and who we are becoming. In classroom drama, pupils are asked to look at how and why people behave as they do both now and in the past, both in cultures like ours and in cultures that are different from ours. They can safely experience the consequences of their actions and 'rehearse' alternatives to behaviours that create conflict, violence or intolerance. They can discuss the rights and wrongs of different actions and examine the links between beliefs, cultural traditions and behaviour.

Anthropologists tell us that drama plays a role in four areas of community life: as education, healing, ritual and entertainment. In the community of the primary school, drama may be used educationally in the sense that it is being used to teach the curriculum or to develop young people's understanding of themselves, others and the worlds in which they live. Drama may also be used for healing – to address and work with those who are bullied, or who are victims of prejudice, or with other concerns and issues that may be negatively impacting on the community of the class or school, such as the reluctance of boys to work with and honour the contributions of girls. Drama is used as ritual whenever we work with a class in drama as a community, whenever, through participating in theatre together, we also learn to be mindful of ourselves, others who are different from us and the world that we all must share. And of course it is equally important that drama is also used in schools purely for entertainment, for fun and for aesthetic pleasure. Any drama programme for a school that ignores the need to be entertaining will not survive for long!

Through drama – as a process of improvement

Drama in the primary years combines two powerful learning processes: story and role play. We are the stories that we tell each other about ourselves and about the world. Stories are at the heart of childhood, from the earliest pre-school years. Fantastical stories give delight and stretch imaginations. Stories about family, community and heritage, stories about how others live here and now, or in other times and other places, will have begun to shape a child's sense of belonging to a particular community and understanding of the world. We continue to use stories as an imaginative resource in school. We use them to create interest in learning history, science and other academic subjects as well as to guide the moral and spiritual growth of the child. Stories give shape to each child's experience, and to the way that they think, express and communicate themselves to others.

There is always a story at the heart of every drama. Sometimes the drama will be based on an existing and well-known story, such as Noah's Ark, a story from the Ramayana, or a picture story book such as *Not Now Bernard* (see p. 52). Sometimes, the class will build a story as they go. The story shape of drama provides a familiar framework for children, which links pre-school learning with the new challenges of academic learning. Because stories appeal to our emotions as well as to our intellects, they combine cognitive and affective learning and allow children to engage with the strangeness of the facts and figures of the world at a feeling level.

'Becoming' the story

In drama we begin a special relationship with stories. Instead of hearing and responding to stories that are happening to someone else, we take on the roles of the characters in the story and imagine that we are now facing the same situations and problems ourselves. In one example, a class was given the subject of villagers facing a drought. Their drama *became* the story of the villagers and what they did to overcome their problems.

'Becoming the story' uses a second 'natural' learning process also – role play. From an early age children learn that the social world is based on role. They see the woman who is in turn a mother, a wife, a citizen, a worker. They begin to recognise that people behave differently according to the social contexts in which they find themselves. They begin to learn that they must adapt their own speech and behaviour according to whether they are at home with their families, in the classroom, in the playground, in places of worship. Children will also have had some experience of using role play as a means of making sense of the adult world, through role playing adults and their behaviour.

We can see this form of play, in which children imagine themselves as adults with adult responsibilities, in the home, in the street and in the playground. Classroom drama harnesses this instinctive learning style to the demands of the curriculum. More often than not, children will take on adult roles in the drama, and this allows them to engage with the curriculum in ways that adults engage with the world. They will become the adults of the village who are responsible for feeding their children; the scientists who may be able to help the villagers with the effects of drought; the neighbours who are asked to share their resources.

At the heart of all drama is this opportunity for role playing, for imagining one-self differently; imagining oneself as the 'villager'; trying to find something of oneself in the role of the 'villager' facing drought and in so doing to recognise the 'villager' in oneself. The problems of the village are not remote concerns – we have imagined for ourselves what it would be like to be in their situation. This self–other recognition is of course important to developing empathy and tolerance of differences. Here Helen, a class teacher, describes the positive effects that role playing can have in causing children to re-examine their own behaviours:

Bullying

Siham was an extremely dominant member of the Year 4 class and had been involved in many situations of bullying and making children feel excluded from the group. She enjoyed a great deal of attention and demanded a lot of positive praise. She was a less able child and found it extremely difficult to work in a group successfully without simply taking over.

To address issues such as this I planned a drama lesson that would explore acceptance and exclusion and the image of bullies and victims. As no real incidences would be referred to, the session was completely non-threatening and was intended to empower children to speak freely.

The children were asked to create a still image based on a scenario given on a card. Siham worked alongside two other boys and two girls, one of whom she had personal difficulties with. Throughout the planning time, Siham was responsive and supportive to her group by sharing and developing her ideas alongside the other children. She didn't dominate or lead in any way but worked as an equal.

The still image that was created was absolutely wonderful. Siham had not only worked successfully within the group, but also portrayed herself as the victim within the group. She was on the floor, crying at the mercy of two bullies. She later explained her role and why she had chosen her specific image, saying that: 'I was being bullied and they had knocked me down. I felt upset because they were hitting me.' Siham was now beginning to show empathy with a victim and this was a way forward, helping her to realise how her own actions impact on the lives of others.

Pupils, in drama, are often asked to take on roles in order to solve problems or dilemmas. They are asked to imagine themselves differently; to reframe or to re-create themselves as 'others':

- ○ *as experts* faced with dilemmas and problems: scientists, builders, archaeologists, doctors, vets, designers, manufacturers;
- ○ *as the powerful,* whose decisions will effect others: policy makers, kings and queens, leaders, generals, superheroes;
- ○ *as transformers of worlds*: peacemakers, landscapers, planners, change agents;
- ○ *as adults exercising adult responsibilities*: teachers, carers, bankers, advertisers;
- ○ *as citizens* negotiating the rules and boundaries of their societies;
- ○ *as parents* caring for their families and the worlds they live in.

Through the kind of empathy work we have described, children can begin to change their ideas about people who are different from themselves. There is an old saying, that once you have truly listened to another person's story you cannot then harm them. In drama we take this one step further by giving pupils the opportunity to do more than merely listen – they experience another person's story for themselves, as if it was their own personal story. Through taking on the roles of leaders, powerful people who can change their lives and circumstances through collective and social action, children may also realise that they can lead, be assertive and change the actual world in which they live. Drama is as we have said, a 'self-realisation' project. It draws out strength, it encourages dreams, and it gives you the chance to reach your potential.

2

From national policy to local practice

This chapter:

o begins with a practical example of drama being used as a means to improve a particular school, Shenton Primary;
o examines the ways in which work at Shenton reflects national policy and guidance;
o draws upon existing documents to find ways of ensuring the quality of the work at Shenton and elsewhere;
o looks at the national guidance on creativity in teaching and learning, and considers what an individual school such as Shenton can learn from this.

Links for all the documents referred to in this section are in Resource 2 on the publisher's website (www.fultonpublishers.co.uk).

Making a policy for drama

In Chapter 1 we concentrated on the 'bigger picture' of drama's role as a school improvement strategy. Now we want to look more closely at the 'real' situation in Shenton Primary, and put it in the context of national policy and guidance. In Chapter 1 we stressed that the focus on drama came from an analysis of the needs of the pupils in a broad sense. These needs related both to improving the quality of classroom learning and also the quality of life in the school. We have argued that drama provides an appropriate way of working on both aspects of the planned improvements in the school – improving learning, improving the quality of life. We also stressed the need to embed drama in every aspect of the life of the school and to encourage staff to work collaboratively in introducing drama in a planned way across the curriculum and across the primary age range. This requires an agreed policy for drama that clearly articulates the aims and rationale for drama, monitoring and assessment arrangements and how progression can be measured.

The Drama Policy is reproduced as Resource 1 on the publisher's website (www.fultonpublishers.co.uk) and is intended to serve as an example of a local policy based on local concerns but also shaped by national policies relating to drama and other relevant aspects of curriculum, pedagogy and assessment. Developing a local policy through collaboration and professional dialogue among all staff involved is an important part of the school improvement-through-drama process and should not be short-circuited by the adoption of external policies that cannot reflect the unique characteristics of your school.

Here Smita, the literacy co-ordinator, describes the context for the creation of the school policy. She emphasises the need for a collaborative and mutually supportive approach; the need to embed drama in other school policies such as the behaviour and teaching and learning policies; and the need to clearly indicate and plan for cross-curricular links made with drama.

> Our school policy stresses that teaching drama is a whole school approach. It enables the whole school and all staff to be involved in using drama. In this way it becomes part of the whole school ethos and emphasises that we are all actively promoting this type of learning. Having a policy framework means that drama is given the same status as all other curriculum subjects. It shows that this form of learning will take place in our school and will be valued; the progress made will be monitored and used to enhance achievement in other curriculum areas. An agreed and negotiated policy framework provides clear guidelines for teachers in terms of the aims of drama, the role of the teacher, the resources available and the monitoring and assessment arrangements. It also outlines the support available from the drama co-ordinator.

> As well as developing a drama policy we revised our Learning and Teaching policy and other key policies in order to include learning and teaching through drama as a way of promoting creativity in children, particularly using cross-curricular links. We also emphasised that through drama children will become active in their own learning.

> We were keen to promote cross-curricular links with other subjects, so we looked at the schemes of work for other subjects and noted the opportunities for teaching a particular topic through drama to enhance creativity and enjoyment of learning.

National policy and guidance

There are two strands of policy documents and guidance which are relevant to school improvement through drama. The first strand contains specific advice on using drama as a learning process in the National Literacy Strategy and the Primary Strategy, as well as advice on teaching drama as an arts subject in its own right as part of all pupils' entitlement to a high quality arts education. This strand is useful in shaping the content and assessment of a drama curriculum based on the principles established in Chapter 1. The second strand contains advice on promoting creativity in teaching and learning and suggests particular teaching and learning styles that can be effectively developed through drama. This strand is useful in identifying the key pedagogic skills and techniques required for effective drama teaching in particular and effective primary years teaching in general. Again our expectation is that by developing the skills and techniques needed for drama, teachers are also developing the quality of cognitive, affective and social learning across the life of the school.

Strand One – Drama objectives and expectations

Statutory requirements for drama in the orders for English in the National Curriculum – DfES/QCA

The programmes of study set out what pupils should be taught in English . . . and provide the basis for planning schemes of work . . . the requirements cover speaking and listening, reading and writing. Some aspects of each are distinctive, but since language development depends on their interrelatedness, teaching needs to build on the links between them.

(The full reference for this can be found on the publisher's website, www.fultonpublishers.co.uk)

Although drama is not a core or foundation subject in the English National Curriculum, there are statutory requirements for drama at Key Stages 1 and 2 contained in the orders for English. These references to drama are the cornerstone of national policy. The other references to drama in National Literacy Strategy and Primary Strategy policy are all based on these statutory requirements and in effect adapt them to the specifics of literacy development and speaking and listening in particular.

The statutory requirements are contained in the orders for English under 'EN1 – Speaking and Listening', there are some additional references to drama in 'EN2 – Reading' and 'EN3 – Writing' as shown in Table 2.1.

The emphasis in these requirements is on linking:

o learning through and about stories with a focus on using drama to explore, present or comment on character, settings and plot;
o learning through and about the dramatic concepts and activities associated with role play, with an emphasis on using language and action to create, adapt and sustain roles/characters suggested by stories.

Table 2.1   Statutory requirements for drama for Key Stages 1 and 2

Key Stage 1	Key Stage 2
To participate in a range of drama activities, pupils should be taught to:	*To participate in a wide range of drama activities and to evaluate their own and others' contributions, pupils should be taught to:*
Use language and actions to explore and convey situations, characters and emotions	Create, adapt and sustain different roles, individually and in groups
Create and sustain roles individually and when working with others	Use character, action and narrative to convey story, themes, emotions, ideas in plays they devise and script
Comment constructively on drama they have watched or in which they have taken part	Use dramatic techniques to explore characters and issues
	Evaluate how they and others have contributed to the overall effectiveness of performances
Drama activities should include:	
Working in-role	
Presenting drama and stories to others	*Drama activities should include:*
Responding to performances	Improvisation and working in-role
	Scripting and performing in plays
	Responding to performances
Reading activities should include:	
Learn, recite and act-out stories and poems	*Reading activities should include:*
Respond imaginatively in different ways to what they read (for example using the characters from a story in drama)	Reading stories, plays and poems aloud
	Writing activities should include:
	A range of forms, such as narratives, poems, playscripts, reports, explanations, opinions, instructions, reviews or commentaries

For this reason, the National Curriculum requirements underpin our model of drama as story plus role play, in which story and role play are both methods of teaching and learning and the subject of teaching about how stories are written and read, how they convey meanings about the world and how drama works through the physical creation of characters and settings. In Chapter 1, we gave reasons why these two processes of story and role play can be powerful tools for cognitive, emotional and social learning.

The National Literacy Strategy (DfES)

Literacy unites the important skills of reading and writing. It also involves speaking and listening which, although they are not separately identified in the National Literacy Strategy Framework, are an essential part of it. Good oral work enhances pupils' understanding of language in both oral and written forms and of the way language can be used to communicate.

The National Literacy Strategy, published by the DfES in 2003, provides schools with a range of teaching objectives for Reception to Year 6 in order to support literacy development. It has been designed to cover the statutory requirements for reading and writing in the National Curriculum Orders for English, while also contributing to the development of pupils' speaking and listening skills. Although it is intended for use within the 'Literacy Hour' on a daily basis it is also relevant for teaching across the entire curriculum.

The core drama-related references in the National Literacy Strategy are given in Table 2.2.

Table 2.2   References to drama in the National Literacy Strategy

Year	Text level objectives
R	**R7**: To use knowledge of familiar texts to re-enact or re-tell to others, recounting the main points in correct sequence
1	**T1/TR7**: To re-enact stories in a variety of ways, eg through role play using dolls or puppets **T2/TR9**: To become aware of character and dialogue, eg by role playing parts when reading aloud stories or plays with others
2	**T2/TR7**: To prepare and re-tell stories individually and through role play in groups, using dialogue and narrative from text
3	**T1/TR3**: To be aware of the different voices in stories using dramatised readings, showing differences between the narrator and different characters used, eg puppets to present stories **T1/TR5**: To recognise the key differences between prose and play script, eg by looking at dialogue, stage directions, layout of text in prose and play scripts **T1/TW14**: To write simple play scripts based on own reading and oral work **T2/TR4**: To choose and prepare poems for performance, identifying appropriate expression, tone, volume and use of voices and other sounds **T2/TR5**: Rehearse and improve performance, taking note of punctuation and meaning

4	**T1/TR5**: To prepare, read and perform play scripts; compare organisation of scripts with stories – how are settings indicated, story-lines made clear? **T1/TR6**: To chart the build up of a play scene, eg how scenes start, how dialogue is expressed, and how scenes are concluded. **T1TW13**: To write play scripts, eg using known stories as basis

5	**T1/TR5**: To understand dramatic convention including
	  o the convention of scripting (eg stage directions, asides)
	  o how character can be communicated in words and gesture
	  o how tension can be built up through pace, silences and delivery

6	**T1/TW9**: To prepare a short section of story as script, using stage directions, location and setting

These references begin to describe the ways in which drama can enrich reading and writing activities in the classroom. Again the emphasis is on bringing stories alive through role playing so that key concepts such as narrative sequence, genre, voice and dialogue can be explored and practised using role play. This may involve the use of dolls and puppets. Dolls and puppets are of course familiar both as legitimate forms of drama, from traditional puppets through to cartoons, and as tools for dramatic role playing in the early years of childhood. Children are also introduced to written forms of drama and the basic conventions of scripting as well as to key concepts in drama such as tension and characterisation using voice and gesture.

Drama in Schools, ACE

Drama has its own history and body of work, much of which has a unique and important place in our cultural life. In common with all subjects, it requires specific skills, knowledge and understanding which are progressively taught and assessed across the key stages.

In 2003, the Arts Council published the second edition of *Drama in Schools* which was intended to fill the gap left by drama's exclusion from the National Curriculum as a subject in its own right. In the absence of any national agreement on drama, many schools are left without the levels of support and guidance offered in National Curriculum subjects. This is a particular problem in Key Stages 3 and 4 when drama is often taught as a separate arts subject rather than as part of English or as part of a whole school, cross-curricular strategy. The emphasis in this document is very much on defining drama as a subject, outlining the key objectives for the study of drama and modelling progression in drama across the key stages. From this point of view, the document offers advice on the drama-specific learning that might be planned for in Key Stages 1 and 2, so that learning through drama in a diverse range of academic and pastoral contexts can be combined with an education in drama as an art form.

Best practice

Drama in Schools (2nd edition) contains descriptions of best practice in the primary years, which are useful indicators for schools, so that their own home-grown policy for drama is benchmarked against expectations produced by an influential national organisation.

Foundation Stage

Pretending to be others in imagined situations and acting out situations or stories are important activities in the dramatic curriculum for the Foundation Stage, as identified by QCA. The imaginative role play area and other play situations provide many opportunities for very young children to experience and develop their early drama skills and knowledge, and to learn about the world.

Drama supports the development of Foundation Stage early learning goals in many ways. Children can suggest their own ideas for planning and creating a role play area. Then, as they play, the teacher or other adult can intervene sensitively as an active participant. This validates and extends the narrative of the play, supports appropriate language and allows the children to explore the power of their roles. Creative drama develops alongside imagination, confidence and language. As children engage in these drama activities they become increasingly aware of the use of space and the way body language communicates meaning.

Again, there is a strong emphasis here on linking story and role play to provide very situational learning in role play areas designed as shops, places of work or environments such as rainforests. The advice also supports our argument that drama is a particularly powerful way of helping young children to learn about the world in the broadest sense through imagining themselves in a variety of real life situations suggested by a story or by the curriculum. There is also encouragement for adults to involve themselves in the make-believe play in order to develop the narrative and create opportunities for language development. Working in-role with children in this way is a particularly important drama strategy, which will be discussed in more detail in Chapter 5.

Key Stages 1 and 2

The opportunity to act out a story to others can be a highlight of the school experience for some pupils, particularly if they find other means of expression more difficult. Primary school pupils benefit from visits to and from theatre companies. This may help them to understand the process of making, performing and responding to plays and provide insights into a range of cross-curricular themes and issues, enhancing the teaching of other subjects, such as history and citizenship.

During Key Stage 1, pupils move from make-believe dramatic play for themselves to a more consciously planned form of drama, which may involve communicating with an audience. Good practice at Key Stage 1 involves pupils in activities such as exploring their ideas through devising scenes. They can work with a 'Teacher-in-role' enacting their own stories for others through small group playmaking, using symbolic 'costumes' and props to stimulate drama narratives. Pupils become increasingly aware of their audience and act out stories using voice, movement, gesture and basic sound effects. When they talk about dramas they have seen or in which they have taken part, they can differentiate between them and explain how effects were achieved.

During Key Stage 2, pupils use a wider range of dramatic devices and techniques. Increased control of voice and body means that they portray more precisely defined characters. Pupils produce work with a clear story-line and structure. They become familiar with forms such as shadow puppets, mime and chorus work, and those in other media, like animation. Pupils may learn lines and write short scripts which grow out of practical exploration of a story. They make connections between broader dramatic traditions and their own work, suggesting improvements. They may also experiment with simple technical effects and equipment, such as digital camera and video.

Drama teaching often explores issues, ideas and dilemmas relevant to pupils' lives and investigates the behaviour of individuals and the nature of relationships. It therefore makes a particular contribution to personal, social and moral education. Drama is a social activity requiring pupils to communicate, co-operate and collaborate. It fosters creativity and thinking skills, raising pupils' self-esteem and confidence through self-expression. These aspects of learning are important for all pupils.

The advice suggests that there should be progression across the Key Stages, from the informal and unstructured use of make-believe play which characterises pre-school and Foundation Stage learning towards the more adult idea of a 'play' which is planned and performed for an audience. We believe that a successful policy for drama in Key Stages 1 and 2 should include both forms of 'play' – the exploratory, risk-taking, inventive and yet uncertain uses of improvised role play, and the careful planning and performance of plays for an audience.

The advice also suggests that children should be introduced to an increasingly broad and sophisticated range of 'devices' and 'techniques' for drama work. These include the use of props and costumes, for instance, as well as techniques, or conventions, for exploratory drama work, such as *hot seating, still images* and *'Teacher-in-role'*. These techniques offer teachers a palette from which to select and plan appropriate means for establishing, developing and reflecting on the drama. We describe the most commonly used and appropriate conventions for primary drama in Resource 6 (on the publisher's website www.fultonpublishers.co.uk) and end Chapter 5 with an extended example of a drama based on the use of appropriately selected drama conventions.

Learning about the world

Once again, the advice from the policy document draws our attention to the important links between story, role play and a wide range of cognitive, affective and social learning. The idea is that drama can play a similar role in the community of the school as it does in the life of society, by representing, commenting on and inviting discussion about the issues and concerns that affect our community life and the world that we share and which our children will inherit.

Hajra, the assistant headteacher, gives us this example of combining story and role play to explore global issues that will have a significant impact on the lives of children as they grow into adulthood.

> I wanted to base my Year 3 drama sessions on something that would encourage children to think and participate on a theme over a period of time. I chose *Oi Get Off My Train* by John Burningham as a starting point because it reflected on environmental issues in a non-threatening form. It was a global issue, not just local. There were challenges for the children about the global issues through the little boy's journey on a train. There were lots of opportunities for cross-curricular work, eg Literacy, Geography and Art. We then extended the work to focus on rainforests and lots of writing and poetry emerged from the drama sessions. Children at the end of the work had a good understanding of the global issues and were able to confidently express their thoughts and ideas. This came through the practical sessions of taking on different roles. Children could express how the animals felt by using vocabulary and language used and introduced in the drama sessions, which they then took back to the classroom and used in their written work. Children took on roles of protestors and campaigners to talk about how they could support the animals over the global issues.

Using the 'story plus role play' approach to explore issues can be a particularly complex activity in urban and diverse schools, but this approach is also a safe and contained way of allowing children to develop and express their views even when there are differences between views held by the different communities that they come from. The drama provides the focus for discussion, the social contract established for drama provides the safe and controlled context for democratic discussion of alternatives, as Dionne, a Year 5 class teacher, explains. She was working on the picture story book *The Conquerors* by David McKee, which tells the story of an all-powerful nation that sets out to conquer the world through force, in order to make these countries 'just like ours'. The full scheme is included in Chapter 6, but here Dionne reflects on her class's learning:

> The initial activities were very specific to the story-line of the *The Conquerors,* however the session took on a global significance, which reflected on international events occurring at the time (the Iraq War). This was eventually brought up by a pupil, during Activity 5, who commented on how this was what the Iraqi people must have felt like when the Americans invaded their country. An overall observation of the session is that children aged only 9 and 10 years old were given the opportunity in which they could express mature, sympathetic opinions on the issues of war, invasion and friendship on a very complex level beyond that of the fictional story-line and characters.

Progression

Drama in Schools includes an assessment framework for drama across all the key stages. This framework usefully suggests what might be expected in terms of pupil achievement at the end of Key Stage 1 and Key Stage 2, and can be used as a benchmark in a local model of progression in drama. The framework is based on three strands of making, performing and responding, which represent the key areas of learning activity in drama in all key stages. The Shenton Drama Policy adopts these three strands as an organising framework for setting out objectives and assessment guidelines.

At the end of Key Stage 1 it is suggested that the majority of pupils will achieve level 2 described in Table 2.3.

Table 2.3 'Three strands' framework for Key Stage 1

Making	Pupils can:
	Take part in a range of drama activities and use simple theatre devices/techniques, eg narration and still image
	Explore problems in an imagined world and make up plays from stories or other stimuli
	Use the dialogue in existing texts as well as create their own
Performing	**Pupils can:**
	Prepare and learn a few lines in their plays
	Add simple theatrical effects such as a sound effect or significant prop to enhance the work they perform to others
	Use their voices and bodies to create characters and atmospheres, employing language appropriate to the role or character, eg adopting a more 'formal' tone when the situation requires it
Responding	**Pupils can:**
	Recognise different kinds of dramas, eg a television 'soap' and their own 'fantasy' play
	Explain in simple terms how atmosphere is created in plays
	Talk about why they made certain decisions in their play and discuss how their work, and that of others, could be improved by more practice or better staging
	Make simple connections between the dramas they experience and their own lives

At the end of Key Stage 2 it is suggested that the majority of pupils will achieve level 4 described in Table 2.4.

Table 2.4 'Three strands' framework for Key Stage 2

Making	Pupils can:
	Work confidently in groups using a range of drama techniques to explore situations and devise dramas for different purposes
	Plan and structure plays that make use of a range of techniques and forms to express their ideas, eg narration in story theatre, mask work, and mime in physical theatre
	Actively interpret the work of playwrights
	Write and perform their own simple scripts, demonstrating an understanding of some correct theatre conventions
	Establish a character, with control over movement and voice
Performing	*Pupils can:*
	Select and operate a range of simple theatre technologies to create the right space for their drama and to enhance their work
	Learn lines, collaborate with others and organise simple presentations
	Experiment with their voices and movement, to create or present different characters in performance
Responding	*Pupils can:*
	Demonstrate an awareness of some theatre traditions from different times and places (eg Kathakali dance drama, Greek or Tudor theatre)
	Discuss the themes or issues in the drama and the way they were presented
	Reflect on and evaluate their own and other pupils' work, suggest improvements and use correct basic theatre terminology
	Comment on how intended effects have been achieved (eg the use of silence)

These Arts Council level descriptions value drama as a performing art more than as a learning process. They focus on pupils' ability to use stage technology, recognise different genres of drama and conventional performances of scripts for example. Teachers may place a different emphasis in drama and want to take into account progress in pupils' social learning in drama as much as their progress in drama-specific learning. In its assessment guidelines, Shenton Primary School included social and artistic learning benchmarks in the three strands of making, performing and responding in order to keep a dual focus on subject learning and the social learning demanded by and developed through drama. These assessment guidelines are included in Chapter 7 (pp. 145–7).

'Creative Generation' (DfES GTEU)

The Gifted and Talented Education Unit (GTEU) of the DfES created this website to support teachers in identifying talented artists and performers. The content is underpinned by the principle that every pupil should be offered opportunities to engage in all the arts, irrespective of ability. The inclusive nature of the arts subjects is to be celebrated. Arts experiences in schools can and do engage all pupils.

'Creative Generation' (www.creativegeneration.co.uk) provides advice on differentiation and extension objectives, which are incorporated into the drama policy and the framework of drama objectives, strategies and examples in Resource 4 (www.fultonpublishers.co.uk). It also suggests performance indicators for identifying potentially talented pupils in drama. These indicators are modelled on those given in the Arts Council's *Drama in Schools* (discussed above) and have informed the shaping of Shenton's own local model of assessment and progression in drama, which is covered in the Appendix on page 157.

The website also includes two statements which can be applied for the benefit of all pupils in drama, on the basis that drama provides a forum both for learning about the world and also for developing certain key skills which are transferable to other domains of life and learning:

> Like all the arts, drama helps both participant and audience make sense of the world. This takes place through the creation and exploration of imagined worlds containing characters and relationships, situations and the events that they encounter (the 'content' of the drama).

> Through engagement with drama activities, pupils apply their imaginations and draw upon emotional memories . . . Drama work enables them to shape, express and share their ideas, feelings and responses through the 'form' of drama.

There is also support in this document for the three generic learning themes which underpin drama as a school improvement strategy:

o the importance of creating high quality social learning experiences for pupils and teachers;
o the importance of developing and applying a broad range of high quality pedagogic and learning techniques and skills;
o the importance to the community of fostering greater empathy, tolerance and respect for difference.

The 'Creative Generation' materials echo these three themes in their definition of learning in drama:

> As well as understanding the language of theatre as part of culture, the process of learning in drama thus provides opportunities for the development of language in all its forms and for understanding aspects of human concerns and relationships.
>
> Pupils learn:
> o to work creatively together, experimenting with ideas and solving problems;
> o to apply thinking skills within very practical contexts;
> o flexibility, empathy and risk-taking.
>
> These are intrinsic to drama practice and are recognised as vitally important in the workplace and throughout adult life.

Primary National Strategy: speaking, listening, learning

> These materials . . . focus on this fundamental aspect of primary classrooms. For some time now, teachers have been asking for more support in the area of speaking and listening to compliment the objectives for reading and writing set out in the National Literacy Strategy Framework for teaching.

This document (produced by DfES in 2003) has been published to support 'a more systematic approach to oral work' through a range of speaking and listening objectives which all teachers are now being encouraged to build in to their teaching. These have been divided into four strands, as shown in Table 2.5.

Table 2.5   Speaking and listening objectives from the Primary National Strategy (DfES 2003)

Speaking	Being able to speak clearly and to develop and sustain ideas in talk
Listening	Developing active listening strategies and critical skills of analysis
Group discussion and interaction	Taking different roles in groups, making a range of contributions and working collaboratively
Drama	Improvising and working in-role, scripting and performing, and responding to performances

The Strategy establishes termly learning objectives for drama incorporating the statutory orders and other National Literacy Strategy guidance. These termly objectives from Years 1 to 6 are designed to lead into the yearly objectives for drama in the National Key Stage 3 Strategy. Together both sets of objectives provide a comprehensive national framework for drama from Years 1 to 9.

These objectives are shaped by two assertions in the primary strategy which were particularly appropriate to Shenton's vision for drama:

1 Drama needs to be explicitly taught in its own right and can also be used as a tool for understanding in subjects across the curriculum.
2 Drama provides many opportunities for children to use heritage languages and knowledge of a range of cultures to experiment with style of speaking, gesture and mime.

In addition to setting out clear objectives for drama, the document also suggests some key techniques for drama and gives advice on how they might be used. These key techniques have been incorporated into the definitions of drama devices and techniques in the appendix.

Staff decided to integrate the primary strategy drama objectives within their agreed whole-school objectives. In other words, they chose to use the primary strategy objectives as the framework for planning drama but wanted to ensure that these external objectives were mediated through the five core objectives for drama that had emerged from staff dialogue and their analysis of their pupils' needs at a local level.

Making Sense of the Primary Strategy Drama Objectives (Resource 4, full details on the publisher's website, www.fultonpublishers.co.uk) was created to provide all classroom teachers across the years with working examples of how to use the objectives. For each termly objective there is a selection of tried and tested strategies, and an example of classroom-based drama activities of work across the curriculum. The document shows how the various fragments of national policy and guidance can be drawn together into examples of actual classroom practice. But the strategies and classroom examples used to demonstrate the objectives in action are also shaped by a careful consideration of which teaching and learning styles are most likely to lead to a more creative curriculum – they are an attempt to move towards a more creative pedagogy through drama.

Strand Two – Towards a creative pedagogy

During the development phase of their school improvement through drama strategy, Shenton School were encouraged by other national initiatives that recognised the importance of creativity in learning, in particular, the OfSTED reports on *The Curriculum in Successful Primary Schools* (2002) and *Excellence and Enjoyment – A Strategy for Primary Schools* (2003). Both these reports conclude that successful schools stress creativity in teaching and learning and described two impacts of this approach:

1 Thinking and behaving creatively brings vitality to learning, providing the motivation to tackle bigger challenges and, when effective, increasing pupils' confidence and self-esteem.

2 Where creativity has an important place in the curriculum, pupils generally have very positive attitudes towards learning and enjoy coming to school.

The staff had begun to feel that they had lost their 'creative' edge. They were conscious that the pressures of delivering an overburdened National Curriculum and using what they considered to be a narrow range of teaching styles in teaching a prescriptive literacy strategy in particular had led to a lack of 'creativity'; not just in terms of allowing the arts to fade into the background, but also in terms of their own personal creativity and that of their pupils. In this sense the project was about 'unlocking' the personal creativities in the school community in order to bring more life into teaching and learning. Drama represented one of the 'bigger challenges' that staff felt they were ready for. Facing this challenge was seen as a way of increasing the confidence and self-esteem of the staff as well as the pupils.

The school was also very concerned to develop positive attitudes towards learning and the school as a 'home' and community resource in the lives of the children. The school wanted to explore more creative ways of addressing the problems that many children had in building and maintaining positive relationships with others who were different in terms of gender and culture in particular. Many pupils lacked confidence and self-esteem and found it difficult to express themselves in a language which was different from their home language. The school wanted to create a learning community based on the principles of respect, tolerance and social responsibility. In doing this, the school was aware that children were sometimes hearing mixed messages about tolerance and respect for other faiths and cultures in particular both in the home and in the madrassa. It was important for the school to try and model, within and for the community, creative ways of living together based on a recognition and a valuing of differences.

In short the drama programme was about learning to lead 'creative lives'. Learning to develop the personal and social creativity needed to adapt successfully to rapid community and cultural change. Developing the skills of flexibility, innovation and risk-taking needed to face uncertain futures and life pathways both in work and in the home and community. Developing the interpersonal and other communication skills as well as the qualities of tolerance and respect needed to find positive and alternative ways of negotiating personal and social conflicts.

Drama can serve these sorts of purposes very well. It is based in 'self-realisation', in the belief that in drama every child should be able to realise their potential whatever their ability or background. It is not a subject which requires particular levels of cognitive ability or physical dexterity – it can be adapted to make the most of the strengths that individuals and groups have. Chapter 3 of this book will detail the kinds of strategies that teachers can use in drama to give value and recognition to pupils' contributions.

Drama is based in the same kind of social contract that establishes the ground rules of rights and responsibilities that underpin the public life of society, so it is a good way of 'rehearsing' democratic living. Drama invites us to imagine ourselves and others differently, to propose and test out alternatives, to imagine how the world can be improved. And of course, drama is in any case a 'creative' activity in the sense that we think and behave imaginatively in order to use what we know about the world to create something which is new and original and of value. This work is always purposeful – it is tied to the need to create a working dramatic context through 'story plus role play'. No two dramas are the same; pupils will make something new out of the ideas that they are offered. And because it is their own work, which has been experienced at an emotional level, it will have added value for pupils and their teachers.

The drama programme was shaped by these concerns and the hope that drama would provide a means of realising a future-orientated curriculum in which children's social, emotional and spiritual needs were in the foreground, which encouraged critical thinking and imaginative responses and a greater sense of 'dialogue' between teachers and between teachers and pupils.

Helen, a Year 4 class teacher, reminds us that:

> With drama you are often reacting to the unknown. You know what your starting point is going to be, but the input comes from the children, and their perspective or view on the stimulus might be very different to how you anticipated it. So you don't quite know where the drama lesson is going to go, how individuals are going to react to it or what feelings it might stir up. It can seem like a snowball and if you sit and think about it too much you'll never do it. Just give it a go!

Samina, a Year 2 learning support assistant (LSA), who takes an active role in drama, witnesses its potential to unlock children's creativity:

> The children really enjoy drama and I feel they are more motivated and interested in the activities when taught in this way. Sometimes the children surprise you as they create really fantastic images with such wonderful expressions. Some children who are quiet in the class or not so confident come out with brilliant ideas. You get to see a different side to them. I enjoy talking to and supporting the children when they are working in small groups to gather ideas or working together to create a still image. They just become so involved in the task. The children now see that drama is just like another lesson, but using a different style, so their behaviour is also good.

A pedagogic framework for creative learning

The two OfSTED reports, together with other guidance on creativity, suggest a pedagogic framework for effective teaching. This framework is particularly suited to drama teaching, but is also essential in all other forms of teaching and learning. Developing the skills and confidence to teach drama effectively using this framework will encourage transferability to other teaching in the school. It will also help pupils to adapt to the challenges of unlocking their own personal creativity, both in the classroom and in the wider community of school and beyond.

Table 2.6   A framework for creative teaching and learning

Questioning and challenging	Asking questions such as 'Why does it happen this way?' or 'What if we tried it that way?'
	Responding to tasks or problems in an unusual way; showing independent thinking
Making connections and seeing relationships	Using analogies; making unusual connections; applying knowledge and experience in a new context
Envisaging what might be	Seeing new possibilities; looking at things in different ways; asking, 'What if?' or 'What else?'
Exploring ideas, keeping options open	Exploring; experimenting; trying fresh approaches; anticipating and overcoming difficulties
Reflecting critically on ideas, actions and outcomes	Reviewing progress; inviting feedback and acting on it; putting forward constructive comments, ideas, and ways of doing things

The framework is applied in drama through the use of a range of appropriate teaching strategies. These strategies are not particular to drama, they can be applied across a variety of teaching and learning contexts, but drama focuses on the need for a wide range of teaching in order to help a class to realise the framework – in order for the children to engage in questioning and challenging, make connections and see relationships, for instance. The range of strategies which staff focused on developing through their drama teaching are laid out in Table 2.7.

Table 2.7   Appropriate teaching strategies for drama work

Direction:	Action:
To ensure pupils know what they are doing, and why	○ Begin each lesson with a clear sense of purpose. What are we learning? Why use drama? ○ Refer to learning objectives throughout the lesson not just at the beginning
Demonstration:	**Action:**
To show pupils how effective an idea, convention, style, etc. can be	○ Use a variety of methods to demonstrate an idea, for example an OHP to show a map of the island or PowerPoint to share photographs of characters which have been created by the group ○ Target individuals or small groups of pupils who you might wish to undertake guided work with
Modelling	**Action:**
To provide pupils with an idea of what is expected and how an activity or task might be approached	○ Select pupils to model good practice. ○ Model good practice both in and out of role. ○ Check that any modelling has been carefully prepared to engage and sustain interest. For example make effective use of space, props, language, registers, etc.
Questioning	**Action:**
To probe, draw out or extend pupils' thinking	○ Encourage pupils to ask questions that will help to understand and make sense of their own and others thinking. ○ Use questions to challenge prejudicial or culturally specific attitudes or ideas. ○ Use questions to affect, extend or alter pupils' understanding; for example, 'What if . . .?' ○ Use questions to draw pupils' attention to the consequences or implications of their actions
Scaffolding	**Action:**
To provide pupils with a series of progressive stages within any given task, helping pupils to build confidence and understanding in their work	○ Consider potential learning outcomes across the ability range when planning for each task. ○ Scaffold each activity with a series of stages, which are clearly identifiable, in order to support individual learning needs and inspire confidence in reaching levels of achievement

(continued)

Table 2.7 *Continued*

Explanation	Action:
To clarify expectations as well as misconceptions and exemplify the best ways of working	○ Keep language simple. ○ Talk with meaning and purpose. ○ Check pupils' responses to and understanding of the explanation; for example, 'Ibrahim can you explain to the class what I have asked you to do?'
Exploration	**Action:**
To encourage critical thinking and generalisation	○ Ensure that lessons are relevant and meaningful to all pupils according to gender, culture, religion, race, etc. ○ Explore material from different viewpoints and perspectives
Investigation	**Action:**
To encourage enquiry and self-help	○ Provide pupils with the ability to draw on a range of dramatic techniques, styles and genres in order to explore and develop enquiry and exploration into their own ideas ○ Encourage pupils to take on roles, which will require them to imagine themselves differently
Discussion	**Action:**
To shape and challenge developing ideas	○ Draw upon and value pupils' own knowledge, ideas and experiences ○ Use discussion to encourage involvement and increase ownership within their work
Reflection and evaluation	**Action:**
To help pupils to learn from experience, successes and mistakes	○ Ensure that reflection takes place during the activity as well as at the end of it. What works? What doesn't? Targets to improve? ○ Encourage pupils to regularly stand back from their work to help deepen their understanding of their own or another's role within it

3

Getting ready for drama

This chapter:

o looks at the key considerations to take into account when preparing for the challenges of drama work;
o discusses how best to contract ground rules for drama work based on negotiation and dialogue with the class;
o suggests some key strategies for managing behaviour in drama and for creating a positive and empowering learning environment;
o gives a behaviour checklist for analysing and reflecting on problems that might emerge in drama;
o presents an example lesson structure, highlighting the use of behaviour strategies in drama.

Being a creative, interactive and social way of learning, drama can offer particular challenges both for teachers and for pupils. It is important not to ignore the difficulties many teachers, even experienced teachers, may encounter when they begin to introduce drama as a regular activity for their class.

Our experience at Shenton has taught us that there are certain key skills and strategies which will help a class to fulfil its potential in drama. While some of these may be familiar, we make no apologies for setting out in detail what works best in creating the necessary pedagogy effective drama work. The advice in this chapter is quite general, however, and should be read alongside the more specific advice on differentiating teaching and learning in drama in Chapter 6 and the guidance on assessment for learning in drama in Chapter 7.

Rachel, a Year 6 class teacher, provides an honest assessment of the concerns that many teachers without drama training will share in the early stages of introducing this way of learning to their classes:

In your own classroom, you know what you can and can't do. So taking yourself and your children into an open space, you wonder how they are going to respond. How are you going to respond? You know, projecting your voice, is every one going to hear you? Are there going to be too many distractions? And thinking what are the children capable of in that space, will it get out of hand? So it's the behaviour that worries you.

At first I didn't know how structured the lesson would have to be so I didn't know how certain children would react to a more active approach to learning. I was particularly worried about the kids who struggle with behaviour during normal lessons and I was really worried about how they would react.

Rachel describes the personal risk she took in taking her class into the 'open space' of drama. Creative teaching and learning has an element of risk about it. In drama as in other forms of creative teaching there is some necessary uncertainty about what will happen, how children will respond, what directions might be taken, what the outcomes of the learning might be. But as professionals, teachers can establish certain limits for the work in order to provide themselves and their classes with the necessary security and trust needed to take risks.

The early days showed that beginning drama could reveal problems in a class which were best dealt with in the classroom setting rather than in drama. For instance, drama work often showed the need for a lot of positive work in the classroom on mixing genders, pupils managing space and resources effectively and responsibly, effective task-led small group work. Staff addressed some of these issues by re-evaluating the role of group work, classroom responsibilities, pairings and seating plans in their mainstream everyday classroom routines. This reinforcement of positive behaviour and attitudes in the classroom helped to prepare children for the challenges of drama work in the 'open space' of the school's drama hall.

The teachers were encouraged to work together to address the challenges highlighted in their drama sessions and to consider whether the same challenges were evident in the classroom. For drama-specific problems, they tried to figure out strategies for ensuring that pupils maintained the same standards of discipline, tolerance and respect (for themselves and for others) in drama as they did in the classroom. For children who find the open space and full sessions of drama too challenging at first, this might mean beginning in the classroom. Drama techniques such as *meetings*, *still images* and *hot seating* can be used in the classroom in literacy and history sessions for instance. This might also mean making the drama work more like routine classroom work by stressing the curriculum knowledge that the drama is based in. We describe a useful strategy for this academic curriculum based drama work in Chapter 5 under the heading of 'Mantle of the Expert'.

Where the challenges which drama exposed were also evident in the classroom, teachers considered ways of targeting specific issues both in the drama sessions and also in the classroom. Where teachers felt that there were shared problems between classes they also looked at school policies and how effective they were in supporting the quality of learning and life in the school.

Part of this collaborative work was to compile the audit of effective learning contexts in Chapter 1, so that there was a shared sense of which learning contexts pupils used effectively and felt comfortable with. This work meant that teachers could help each other to identify actions to be taken in both the classroom and in drama. The school improvement through drama programme was aimed at improving the quality of staff relationships as well as those among pupils, and the honest and frank debriefing sessions shared after drama work were key to the successful implementation of the drama policy.

Here Helen, a Year 4 classroom teacher, reflects on her own concerns when facing up to the 'big challenge' of drama and some of the uncertainties she experienced. She outlines her approach, which was to work on key areas of behaviour management outside of the drama time and to use her existing planning skills to prepare for the unexpected:

> I had several concerns in using drama. I felt that there would be behaviour issues in terms of children not co-operating successfully with each other: children not being able to share their ideas, not respecting personal space and not managing their own behaviours within smaller groups. I was also concerned about introducing a new learning style that involved the children working in a new space outside of the classroom. I felt that I would not be prepared for the unknown or where to take the drama lesson, if my plans did not have the expected outcome.

> To address the issue of children working together, I made a conscious decision to expose my pupils to different working groups outside of drama. This way they were familiar with one another and I was able to mix genders and abilities freely. Even a simple routine such as lining up filtered down from drama and became a tool for addressing acceptance of others. Children lined up boy/girl or next to a member of another group and this was reflected in drama when they were often put into an unfamiliar grouping. Circle time was another important aspect that I used in the classroom as a positive step towards turn-taking when speaking and developing listening skills (eg holding the pen and taking turns to speak).

> In relation to expecting the unexpected, I ensured that my planning for drama was thorough and often included more than enough activities that linked together in case adjustments were necessary. I learnt to relax, as the unexpected events and experiences that evolved through the drama activities were often the best moments.

Helen's list of concerns are a reminder of some of the particular challenges that come with drama. Even when drama is done in the classroom, there will need to be some rearrangement of the space, which can disrupt the routines of classroom management for some pupils. Moving into the hall for drama requires pupils to make a disciplined use of the space and of their bodies. Drama work is likely to be more physically and vocally interactive than in some other lessons and will undoubtedly raise social, cultural and personal issues and discussion that might be challenging to respond to. In drama, learning outcomes are less predictable than in some other teaching approaches and teachers need, as Helen recognises, to be flexible in terms of plans and expectations.

The behavioural, emotional or social problems, which you might struggle with in your everyday practice, are likely to be magnified when you begin drama work. But don't be afraid! To have these problems exaggerated in this way will enable you to develop strategies for effectively managing them. However, like all good practice this does not happen overnight. There are no short-term fixes, no instant solutions. Effective behaviour management is developed over time, through the consistency of routine, of rules, of language, both spoken and physical, and through continued reflection on your own practice.

Establishing the ground rules for effective drama work

At the heart of managing new demands made by drama is the idea of a contract, which is a negotiated statement of the ground rules that all class members and their teacher will adopt as a 'constitution' for the class. A central feature of drama work is that it is based on negotiation and dialogue between learners and their teacher. Children cannot in any case be forced to do drama, so there must be some negotiation in order to gain their willing and active consent to join the drama. This agreement to do drama, between pupils and between the teacher and pupils, is easier to make if there is a visible and negotiable framework of ground rules and behavioural objectives. Knowing what to expect from others and what is expected of them gives pupils confidence, security and protection. Knowing what the rules are and what happens if you or others break them makes everyone feel secure.

Because the contract is a social agreement to behave in certain ways, it is everybody's responsibility to uphold it. Everyone who is involved needs to be active in discussing and wording the contract and deciding what sanctions and rewards will support it. When the contract is broken the whole class should be involved in deciding what should be done. It is not just the teacher's responsibility; it is a community responsibility shared by all.

Helen describes how she negotiated the contract for her class and the impact it has had on their learning in general:

When negotiating the rules for our drama sessions, I wanted the children to have as much ownership as possible over them and to support the contract by taking responsibility for their own learning. The rules would act as an agreement between myself, the class and each other, which we would enter into every time we came to work in the drama space.

Initially when the children were asked to suggest rules for their drama activities they were able to think of the basic rules associated with speaking and listening, eg raise your hand before you speak, and listen to the teacher. With prompting and questioning, their ideas developed and I felt able to introduce the terms 'compromise' and 'negotiate'. We also established rules for how we would move in the space and value everyone as equal.

Through discussion and drama practice these rules have gradually become embedded in the children and the impact outside of the classroom has been immense. These rules can be applied so easily to any area of the curriculum to address issues of equality, acceptance and independence, and because the children themselves have devised the rules they feel all the more empowered to use and apply them.

Children need to learn that 'drama', like other areas of the curriculum, is a rule-bound activity, therefore it is essential before beginning drama work with an inexperienced class that quality time is spent working collaboratively to establish a contract, which will enable each individual:

○ to feel safe;
○ to learn without disruption;
○ to know what is expected from themselves;
○ to know what is expected from those around them;
○ to be given confidence;
○ to be given protection;
○ to be treated equally.

The content of the contract should be negotiated through carefully led dialogue. Helen's experiences show that pupils can benefit immensely from being included in such decision-making, as this helps to initiate the beginnings of:

○ ownership for behaviour management;
○ trust among the class;
○ responsibility for one another.

In discussing their experiences of contracting with their classes, the staff identified these steps:

Five positive steps towards creating a 'behaviour' contract

Step 1   Ensure that there is a dialogue between yourself and your pupils while establishing the contract

Step 2   Ensure that pupils feel a sense of ownership in making their classroom a safe, fun and effective learning environment

Step 3   Keep the language positive. Stress what you want pupils to '*do*', not what you '*don't*' want them to do

Step 4   Keep the language used in the contract clear and concise

Step 5   Display the contract clearly in the classroom and drama space and return to it when necessary

---

Figure 3.1   Creating a behaviour contract

This is the Key Stage 1 and 2 contract created by pupils and staff. Classes used this as a starting point for developing their own specific class contract based on discussion and negotiating the wording. Both the rules and sanctions are clearly identified, and were developed with a sound knowledge of the school's current policy on behaviour as well as the system of rewards that accompany this. Rewards take the form of stickers, certificates, letters home, a record in the special mention book (kept in the foyer) and assemblies for sharing positive progress in both subject and social development.

The Famous Five at Shenton Primary School

1   Treat others as you would want to be treated

2   Listen to and follow instructions carefully

3   Keep your hands and feet to yourself

4   Put your hand up when you want to speak

5   Do your best and have a go!

If you can't follow the five:

o   You will be given a verbal warning

o   You will be given a 2-minute time out

o   You will lose 'golden time'

Figure 3.2   'Famous Five' at Shenton Primary School

Pupils designed their own 'symbols' or illustrations for each of their rules. This was particularly important for EAL pupils and those with particular literacy and cognitive difficulties.

We have stressed that drama is a 'self-realisation' project – that by working socially, using the familiar processes of 'story plus role play', pupils across the ability range can realise their potential. A class works together in drama, and must make use of all the strengths in the group. This will often mean that children will have to 're-value' their classmates by putting aside prejudices and gender loyalties that have developed over time. Negotiating and maintaining the class contract provides a process and a benchmark for the whole class to become a more effective, tolerant and responsible unit for social learning.

Creating a positive climate for drama work

Rachel, a Year 5 class teacher, describes some of the gender-specific difficulties she had with a class both in and out of drama. She reinforces our point that problems with a long history, in this case reaching back to the nursery years, will tend to be magnified in drama. This can be unsettling, but with perseverance and support change through drama begins to happen. In this case the combination of the contracting process, the value given to the class in selecting their contract for the school, and a balanced use of some familiar pedagogic skills, drama skills and techniques proved to be effective.

In my experience boys would never work with girls and vice versa. Both sexes were extremely argumentative, which would often interrupt lessons. I found that I was managing fights and negative behaviour and not teaching! Group work, even single-sex groups raised numerous problems as the children had limited experience of compromising and very poor social skills. Personal space was also an issue, once invaded this would cause work to stop and arguments among pupils.

Within the class, there was a collection of strong-willed boys who were constantly fighting over their power position within the class. Then a group of girls had similar problems, including some issues of race. In Year 5 we began to focus on our drama work, partly in the hope that these issues might be addressed through the work. To begin with, the usual power games still played a huge part and progress was extremely slow. There were times where we felt like giving up – but we didn't!

The girls were very separate from the boys and they wanted it to stay that way. Bear in mind that is how they had worked together since Nursery. When they moved up to Year 6, the struggles within the class were such a problem that work was being seriously hindered. So we decided to tackle this problem through drama again. We were determined that it was going to work.

Once we started to do drama regularly I began to establish clear guidelines for the children. The class were given the responsibility of designing the '5 drama rules', which they thoroughly enjoyed! So they set the scene for themselves. This seemed to create a new platform for the children to work from. After lots of hard work the changes began to happen and slowly they transferred into the classroom environment.

The contract helps to establish some consistency in what is expected and how problems will be dealt with. But it is important to introduce routine ways of working in drama to help pupils keep to their agreed contract and give sessions a recognisable structure. In the first phase of introducing drama, staff identified certain routines in the pedagogy of drama, which over time began to make a difference. Some of these features were familiar of course from other teaching and learning contexts – others were introduced by the consultant when modelling good drama practice for class teachers and their pupils. These are the routines which staff identified:

Use of space (see also 'Making the space safe', pp. 126–7)

Pupils are already familiar with using alternative spaces for learning outside of the classroom: the hall for assemblies, for PE and/or dance and the playground for mathematical exercises or scientific experiments. Therefore there is an understanding that different activities in different spaces will make different demands on their ability to adapt and change behaviour according to the environment that they are in. Before beginning any drama work the teacher needs to anticipate the problems that might be created by the pupils' use of space. For example:

- if it is messy, disorganised and neglected pupils will respond accordingly;
- begin practical work with a formal use of the space; have the class enter and sit in a formal circle of chairs (or on the floor) or have groups of chairs pre-arranged if the lesson begins with group work;
- establish clear boundaries for group work; place the groups yourself so that they are not too crowded or too distant; make corners, levels and dangerous space off-limits;
- insist on the class working within the space that has been allocated so that they don't interfere with other groups.

The circle (see also 'The circle as a symbol of common unity', p. 127)

Drama begins and ends in a circle, therefore everyone can be seen by one another and there is a sense of equality, particularly if the teacher sits on the floor in the circle with the pupils. If there are problems in the circle, ie pupils sitting behind others, gaps being created to avoid girls, boys or a particular individual, gaps not being created to allow others into the circle, then there will be problems later. Working at getting the circle right will have a positive effect on the work that follows; ignore the gaps and these will continue to reappear in all aspects of the work. These strategies can be useful in establishing the idea of the circle with a class:

o Before making the circle always remind the class of the importance of starting the work in this way.

o Make a circle while everyone is standing holding hands and then sit when the shape is organised with everyone involved.

o Enter the space in a 'follow the leader' style. Chose someone sensible to lead the way and ask them to stop once the circle has been formed.

o For younger children build entry into the circle as part of the story; ie, in a hushed voice, 'We're going into the woods today and we must be careful not to frighten the animals. They have been having some problems with humans and we don't want to add to them. So we need to go very slowly and very quietly.' You might want to select someone to lead the group to check that the path is clear and someone to follow from behind to check that everyone stays together.

o Use individual carpet squares, pre-arranged in a circle for pupils to sit on and stay on.

Initiating 'talk'

It is important to initiate 'talk' among all of the pupils. In the open space of drama it is easy to end up relying on the same hands going up in response to a question. The teacher needs routine strategies for incorporating those who might be less confident in the drama space or have simply got into the habit of 'being invisible'. For example:

o *Talk partners* allow time for individuals to talk quietly with the person next to them in order to generate shared responses before feeding back into the group.

o *Target differentiated questions* to individuals. Pupils will listen more effectively when they know that there are questions for everyone to answer.

o *Group thought-showers* are an effective way to pool ideas before sharing them with the rest of the class.

o *Progress partners* are like talk partners but focused on peer-assessment of drama work (see pp. 151–2).

o 'No hands' policy allows thinking time for everyone to prepare a response.

Strategies suggested by the *Primary National Strategy*

The *Primary National Strategy* outlines a variety of strategies that can be used creatively across the curriculum in order to support pupils' development in speaking and listening. Here are some examples:

Glove puppets and shadow theatre

Puppets can be used by children to make and tell stories. Providing a tape recorder while children are rehearsing or developing the script helps them to go through an oral drafting process and understand how they develop and refine the story.

Children can reflect on their use of language and voices. These techniques can also be used to explain, instruct or inform.

Word tennis

This is a way of making a story with a partner, and emphasises listening for key words, main points and events, focusing on the need to make sense. Each person says one word or phrase in turn so that the story is continually passed backwards and forwards. For example: once/there/was/a/queen/who/wanted/to/fly/so/she/sent/for . . .

Think-pair-share

Children are asked to consider an issue or problem individually, such as reading and preparing a response to an information text, or preparing a news item to be read aloud. They then explain their ideas to a partner. After the pairs have discussed the issue, they may join another pair, share views and emerge with a group conclusion or perspective.

Flashbacks and flash forwards

These strategies are effective for getting children to focus on the consequences of action rather than on the action itself. They help avoid the full-scale battle scene, for example! They encourage reflection and discussion. They stop the dramatic action and require the children to refocus on something that happened before, which may have caused a particular event, or happened later, or perhaps as a consequence of the action. Other strategies such as freeze frames may be used to create the flashback from the perspective of different characters.

These strategies and more like them can be found at www.dfes.gov.uk.

Asking the right questions

Questions in drama, as in all other areas of learning, have different functions; ie to open discussion, to reflect on an issue, to provoke action, to test, recall or focus attention: the list goes on.

In drama, the teacher works alongside the pupils, using questions to discover the sense they are making of the dramatic experience. The teacher cannot know what individuals think, how they respond, what connections they are making with their own experience or what ideas they might want to try out without asking! There must be a genuine attempt by the teacher to see the dramatic experience from the pupils' perspective.

In order to make their own questioning more effective, teachers focus on getting pupils to recognise that the wording of questions is an important clue about what is being asked for in terms of a response. Teachers then make consistent use of particular wording in their questions to help the pupils find effective responses. This is the advice that is used with pupils in Key Stage 2:

1 Your teacher will be constantly asking you questions during the drama. These are real questions and the teacher needs your answers in order to decide what to do next in the drama.
2 Listen carefully to the questions asked: sometimes the first word of the question will give you a clue about the kind of information the teacher needs from you.
3 Work out which of these questions is being asked and then help the teacher with a good and useful answer.

For instance:

o *What?* asks you to itemise or list: What do you need? What is X scared of? What will his daughter say when she finds out?
o *When/where/which?* asks you for specific information: When is this happening? Where would she sit? Which of these two chairs would make the best throne?
o *How?* asks you to explain processes and share feelings: How are agreements made in this family? How would she feel about what he is doing? How can we make an image based on that idea?
o *Could/would?* tests your potential: Would she still come back after all she has heard? Would you behave in the same way yourself? Could you imagine that it might be different?
o *Should?* asks you for a moral judgement: Should he have spoken to his mother in that way? Should anyone make that demand on another? Should we try and listen to each other?
o *Why?* asks you for explanations: Why doesn't she answer the question? Why is the king so angry with his daughters? Why are you finding it so difficult to play the character?

Group work

The teacher needs to structure the session so that there are regular opportunities to work in mixed ability and mixed gender groups. Groups that are based on the security of friendship, or that reinforce gender divisions, should obviously be avoided. Staff introduced pupils to these sets of 'rules' for group work at Key Stage 1 and 2.

Key Stage 1

1 Take it in turns to speak.
2 Use each other's names when we speak to or about each other.
3 Listen carefully to each other's ideas.

4 Find out what we agree on.
5 Put ideas into action!

Key Stage 2

1 Make sure we listen to and include everyone in the group.
2 Don't talk over each other.
3 Question! Discuss! Agree! Act!
4 Share out responsibilities.
5 Remember, success is achieved when we work together.

Sharing good practice

While pupils are working independently or in small groups the teacher should select work that can be modelled to the rest of the class. This should be done during the planning and rehearsal stage, so all pupils have the benefit of good ideas to include in their own work as it develops towards performance for the class. Sharing good practice underlines the social nature of drama work; pupils are not competing with each other – they are sharing their best work in order to help others and gain from others.

Sharing good practice also:

○ demonstrates to the pupils that you take time to observe their work;
○ adds value to the tasks set;
○ makes the learning more meaningful;
○ provides other pupils with ideas/clear examples/an idea of the standards that they should be aiming for in their own work;
○ reinforces positive attitudes to learning.

Sharing work

Sharing group or individual work within the class can be made more effective if pupils become familiar with the following routines for performance:

○ using an instrument or a countdown (3, 2, 1) to indicate when the work should begin;
○ asking a volunteer to remind the class how an audience should behave: be silent, listen and watch closely, be ready to say what you liked in the work;
○ reminding pupils that all of their shared work should begin and end with a still image to indicate the start and finish of their work, or as one group melts to the ground another group should slowly get up into position to start, and so on until the last group melts to the floor;
○ sharing work in the space in which the group rehearsed: avoid making groups perform in the centre of the space as this can confuse and threaten some individuals as well as prompting unnecessary movement from everyone;

o using the 'traffic lights' assessment for learning strategy described in Chapter 7 (p. 152).

Celebrating achievement

Drama can be a powerful means for both teachers and children to learn about themselves. It maximises strengths and does not depend for success on differentiated cognitive or physical abilities. It is an area of school life in which every child should be given the chance to excel on an equal footing. For these reasons it is important to celebrate pupils' achievements in their drama work whenever possible. This can be done through assemblies, performances and/or simply by creating displays of their work in drama around the school. Each of these are effective ways to share success and enjoyment among other members of staff, parents, governors and other visitors to the school. They are also a powerful means of raising personal and collective self-esteem.

Valuing pupils' ideas and knowledge

Because drama is a social learning activity that should include the childrens' ideas and thinking as well as the teacher's, it is important for the teacher to take time and effort to value and draw upon pupils' ideas and prior knowledge. This might include making mental notes of responses made by pupils during the drama work and then considering how these can be fed into the drama in later sessions or followed up in the classroom. This will encourage a greater sense of ownership of the work through more sincere and meaningful engagement with the themes and issues raised by the drama.

Reinforcing positive behaviour

When difficulties like those identified by Rachel come out in the drama work, the teacher should take care to single out those pupils who have either listened well, contributed positively, supported other members of the class, acted imaginatively or communicated effectively. It is surprising what impact this has on those pupils who exhibit negative behaviours because they would also like to receive praise. It helps everyone to focus on positive behaviour and attitudes rather than focusing all of the teacher's energies on those pupils who present more challenging problems.

Dealing with disruptive individuals in drama can become a real 'drama' because the whole class can be distracted into being an 'audience', which of course will draw everyone's attention to the teacher's confrontation of the behaviour. It will give weight to the 'incident' as well as disrupting the lesson for the rest of the class.

Strategies for dealing with disruptive pupils include the following:

○ Manage behavioural problems away from the individual's friends.
○ Ensure that the pupil is given clear choices.
○ Ensure that the pupil understands the consequences of his or her choices.
○ Praise the pupil for any positive behaviour that you have seen during the lesson.
○ Ensure that the learning for the rest of the class is not disrupted.

'Acting the teacher' and routines for classroom management in drama

So far, we have described how familiar pedagogic skills and techniques can be used to effect in drama work. However, there are some core drama pedagogy strategies that teachers were introduced to and found useful for helping pupils to make their behaviour purposeful and sensitive to the needs of others.

Drama can of course happen in the classroom, but when the class moves into a bigger and freer space like the studio, both space and the teacher's own use of voice and other aspects of his or her physicality become very important tools for managing behaviour positively.

All teaching is performative: we take on the professional persona of teacher which is not necessarily the same as our other more private persona. In my own life, I tend to be shy and quiet, but as a teacher I know that I must project a more confident and indeed extrovert persona in order to establish my authority in the classroom. We take this kind of professional 'role playing' for granted and may not even be aware that we are acting by controlling our voice and other gestures in order to 'play' the teacher. In drama we can make good use of our role playing skills to maintain a positive climate for drama.

Here are some of the strategies and considerations staff found useful when working in the drama studio and which they recommend as advice to others. They also describe the five techniques that are routinely used in drama for behaviour management.

Commanding the space

Be aware of what impact your presence can make in a space without saying a word. This is particularly important when working in large open spaces. Take command of the space by keeping active in it. Ensure that everyone is able to see and hear you clearly at all times. Controlling the space also means defining which areas the pupils can use in any given activity and which areas and equipment are out of bounds.

As soon as you become aware of a problem emerging, move close to the 'root' of the problem and deliver the lesson from there. Simple, targeted movements or gestures can diffuse all kinds of difficulties. By noticing and moving near to the 'problem' the pupil is more inclined to correct their behaviour without having to be told and the lesson moves on without interruption.

Body language

Again body language is an important device for communicating how you are feeling; it can help add meaning to what you are saying and or implying as well as reinforcing a particular impression that you want to give. In large spaces, it is often necessary to exaggerate body language slightly in order to communicate effectively with the whole class. The following may be helpful:

o Create a range of 'postures', which pupils can become familiar with, so that they understand certain expectations without a word being spoken; eg standing still with arms folded looking at the person(s) you want to signal attention from, or resting your hand across your mouth or chin as if to signal your puzzlement or confusion over a particular action, or a lowered head to signal disappointment.
o Ensure that you are never static for too long. An animated teacher is usually more interesting to engage with or focus on.

Use of voice

While raising your voice can be effective, shouting (particularly in a large space) will only exhaust you. It will also heighten the emotions of everyone involved, create confrontation, possibly entertain those watching, and suggest to the pupils that you are losing control.

o Keep a calm and consistent voice when dealing with difficult behaviour.
o Develop a 'range' of voices which indicate a variety of moods and meanings, eg surprise, disappointment, celebration, pride, etc. In time pupils should be able to recognise and respond appropriately to the sound of your voice and the meaning conveyed by this without further explanation.
o Use clear inflections at the end of sentences to signal the response you want from the class – up for questions, even for statements, down for commands.

Eye contact

A 'look' across the room can speak volumes and not a word has to be said. If you become aware of a potential problem, let the individuals know you know by, firstly, casting a warning 'glance' in their direction. Keep your eyes moving around the room and on each individual. This can help children maintain focus and feel a greater sense of protection by knowing that you are watching closely!

Three useful techniques for classroom management in drama

One – The countdown

Use your fingers to count down (5, 4, 3, 2, 1):

5 Stop what you are doing.
4 Stop what you are saying.
3 Put down what is in your hands.
2 Turn and face the teacher.
1 Be ready to listen.

Alternatively, with younger pupils, you might want to use a drum roll or the jangle of bells to indicate that you want everyone to stop what they are doing and listen to you. This is a useful device that isolates those individuals or groups who are not listening without you having to say a word.

Two – 'Eyes on me'

Before addressing the class, make sure you have everyone looking at you. Remind the pupils that when they hear the words 'Eyes on me', they should turn to face you. Don't begin until you have everyone's attention.

Three – Managing with sound

Instruments can be used effectively as an alternative to the sound of your voice in managing pupil behaviour. Use a drum to indicate transitions and/or changes from one pupil, action, freeze and/or group, etc to another. Use a drum roll or bells to indicate time to get into positions. This could be developed further by using recorded music to:

○ work alongside to, as an additional stimulus;
○ indicate the beginning and end of a scene;
○ add to or create an atmosphere as pupils enter the lesson.

A behaviour checklist

In order to guide and focus discussions about classroom management in drama, staff devised a simple checklist for diagnosing and reflecting together on what happened and what might be anticipated in planning for the next session.

Table 3.1 Learning to behave checklist

	Yes/No	Comment
Did I select models of appropriate behaviour to share with the class?		
Did I offer praise where appropriate?		
Did I take time at the beginning and end of lessons to reflect on whole class/individual progress?		
Were ground rules, codes of conduct and behavioural objectives agreed together?		
Was the contract displayed clearly on the wall?*		
Did I make pupils aware of both the rewards and sanctions that would be applied to particular behaviours?		
Were rewards and sanctions consistent with particular behaviours?		
Did I use the reward system to highlight positive models of behaviour?		
Did I implement the school's policy on behaviour with effect?		
Was I able to apply rules consistently on behaviour?		

* The agreed contract can be used as a reference for pupils when their behaviour becomes inappropriate. It acts as a mediator by stating the facts and reinforcing what is expected and has been agreed previously between the teacher and the pupil.

Applying behaviour strategies in a practical example

With these preparatory considerations in mind, and assuming that there is now a regular dialogue about drama and the expectations that both the teacher and class have, we will now look at what might happen in the first drama lesson. Although this lesson follows a plan, in practice the teacher will need to be ready to think 'on her feet'. Because drama works with both the positive and less positive behaviours of the class, there will always be a big difference between what is planned and the lived experience of the lesson itself. We have suggested that risk-taking in drama needs to be informed by professional judgements, and in time experience will help the teacher to anticipate likely outcomes when planning and also equip the teacher with strategies for responding to the unexpected during the lesson.

Not Now Bernard by David McKee: a sequence of drama tasks

Rationale

This drama session was part of a unit of work for Year 2 pupils on 'understanding character'. Other stories explored alongside this text were *Leola and the Honeybears* and *The Fisherman's Wife* (see Resource 2, on the publisher's website, www.fultonpublishers.co.uk). This work became the focus of a Key Stage 1 assembly whereby the class presented their understanding of character through performance.

Introduction: the whole story

The lesson begins with the class making a circle before sitting down. Explain that you are going to be working with the story *Not Now Bernard*. Some might already be familiar with the story; even so, ask everyone to listen carefully and to remember the different jobs that Bernard's parents were busy with and what Bernard was trying to tell them.

Table 3.2   Introduction: management issues

Children rush into the space and run around	Back to the classroom! Remind pupils that the rules of the classroom apply in the hall. Then enter again
The circle is divided into boys and girls and or cultural groups	Discuss the importance of integrating and working together. Give the class the chance to re-seat themselves, then place pupils yourself and keep to this arrangement until class say they are ready to mix for themselves
Individuals disrupt others who are trying to listen	Stop and address the contract; sit with those who are having difficulty; keep persistent offenders next to you until they learn not to disrupt others
Child is upset by the monster eating Bernard	Protect the child by admitting to your own 'upset' about what happens to Bernard. Ask other pupils to explain why they are not upset by it. Remind them that it is only a story. Discuss whether monsters like the one in the picture really exist

Task 1: We're too busy!

Ask the class to identify, and make a list of:

o the activities that Bernard's parents do to avoid listening to Bernard, eg *hammering*, *cleaning*, *watering the plant*, *painting* and *reading the paper* and ask the pupils for other examples of what the parents might do;
o the feelings expressed on the faces of the characters, eg *anger*, *boredom*, *sadness*.

Explain that the class are going to play a game. Ask for a volunteer to come into the circle to represent Bernard. Everyone on the outside of the circle will work 'in-role' as one of Bernard's parents and must choose one activity and one feeling to express from the lists. The pupil playing Bernard must go up to individuals in the circle and say the following:

'There is a monster in the garden and it's going to eat me!'

Table 3.3   Task 1: management issues

No one volunteers	Offer to work with a volunteer or allow a pair to do the work. Model yourself what needs to be done to show that it is safe to take the risk
Other children laugh at the volunteer	Stop and assess whether the laughter is 'innocent'; if not make it absolutely clear that making others feel uncomfortable is unacceptable behaviour. Offer the chance for an apology. If this chance is not taken, the child should sit out until ready to agree to the contract
The volunteer refuses to work with girls	Again this is unacceptable. There needs to be discussion about how we don't work just with our friends – as in drama as in life. Ask another boy pupil to work with the girl as a role model. Partner the girl yourself and make a point about girl power!
Individuals use this as an opportunity for inappropriate or attention-seeking behaviour	It might be more appropriate to ignore the behaviour to begin with as this is often a sign of insecurity and self-consciousness. If this continues ask the individual to come and stand next to you – this way you can have a quiet word without allowing him or her to interrupt the lesson
A pupil freezes and cannot give a response	Reassure the pupil. Give another chance. Ask what he or she had planned. Model how to do it and allow pupil to repeat

Each individual replies: 'Not now Bernard, I'm busy!' and mimes what activity they are busy with. They then turn to face outwards with their back to Bernard but still showing their chosen feeling. Once everyone's back is turned the activity is complete and Bernard should be left standing alone in the circle.

Task 2: How does it feel?

Sit the class back down in the circle and ask the person in the middle how this must have made Bernard feel when everyone was busy. Ask everyone sitting in the circle to position themselves using *still image* to show how Bernard might be feeling as a result of what has just happened to him. Then ask for a volunteer or the person who has been playing Bernard to move around each image of Bernard. Their task is to *thought-track* some and/or all of the images of Bernard and to speak Bernard's thoughts 'as if' they were Bernard themselves. For example:

'I feel alone and ignored', 'I feel angry that no one would listen'.

Table 3.4 Task 2: management issues

Individuals find it difficult to sit still and maintain their image of Bernard	Stop, countdown from five for a freeze, offer verbal encouragement to anyone who looks as if they are losing concentration, move closer to pupils having difficulty and lightly hold them still and then release
The volunteer struggles to come up with responses	Use questioning to scaffold the task – What might he be thinking? Might he be happy? Why not? How can we put that into words? Imagine that you were Bernard: now speak the words in Bernard's voice
The volunteer uses the third person or description rather than first-person 'thoughts'	Repeat in the first person after each 'thought', stop and encourage, model the difference and try again. Ask a volunteer to help speak the thoughts the volunteer suggests

Task 3: Making a monster

Ask the class to re-tell what happens to Bernard when he meets the monster he has been so worried about. Look again at the picture of Bernard with the monster in the garden.

Ask everyone in the circle to find a partner and label themselves 'A' or 'B'. 'A' must sculpt 'B' into an image of a very scary monster. Remind the pupils that they must consider:

○ what *expression* the monster might have when he tries to get the attention of
   Bernard's parents;
○ how the monster's *body* might be positioned;
○ what the monster's *hands* might be doing.

Pupils swap roles and repeat.

Table 3.5 Task 3: management issues

Pupils are rough with their partners	Add the rule that 'A' must only mirror 'B's' actions. When they have demonstrated this successfully, praise their actions and then if time they can have another go at 'hands-on' sculpting
There is reluctance about touching/being touched	Model the work with the reluctant pupil to demonstrate what is expected. Ask the pupil to explain their reasons and discuss with them. As a compromise, if this continues to be difficult, use mirroring as above
'Monsters' find it difficult to be still or go on the 'rampage'!	Allow movement but control it by using a ten to one countdown in which the monsters can move in 'slow motion' and must then freeze on your command. Use the sanctions in place and give a verbal warning if necessary. If it is one person in particular then take time to model good practice around the class by partnering the individual concerned

Task 4: Monster images

Ask each of the 'B's to come and form a small circle standing and facing outwards. The 'A's then make a surrounding circle facing their partner. Explain to the
class that each time you bang the drum, As must get into position as the monster
and freeze. On the next bang of the drum they must move from their partner to
face the next person in the circle and freeze in their position of the monster. This
activity is repeated until everyone has seen each of the monsters.

   Target individuals to find out which monsters they thought were scary and why.

Task 5: Story board

In five groups, create a physical picture story board using still images to show what
the monster did while he was alone and ignored by Bernard's parents. Groups must
consider how they can use each other to create the objects which might also be in
the image – for example, the TV, a robot, furniture in Bernard's bedroom.

Table 3.6   Task 4: management issues

Individuals are confused about the instructions	Scaffold instructions into manageable stages. Target pupils to recall the instruction as they are given, ie 'A's make a circle or turn and face outwards; 'B's come and stand in front of your partner, etc.
'A's get too close or try to physically antagonise the 'B's	Alter the distance between all of the 'A's and 'B's. Use a piece of fabric and/or beanbags if necessary to mark out the distance between the actor and audience. If someone oversteps the markers they will be asked to sit out
Pupils choose their own work to comment on rather than others	Explain before the task is set that everyone must select someone else's work to comment on beside their own. This could be the work of their 'progress partner' (p. 151)
Pupils get upset because their monster is not chosen as the scariest	Explain that everyone will react differently to the monsters. Give examples of different 'scary' features from within the group

The monster:

1 ate dinner;
2 watched the television;
3 read a comic;
4 broke one of Bernard's toys;
5 went upstairs to bed alone with his teddy.

Each group shares their work and discusses how the monster would have felt about his day at Bernard's house.

Select one image to work with and ask volunteers to change the monster figure into Bernard doing the same activity: watching TV for instance. The point is to help the class realise that Bernard was also lonely and needing some attention. Discuss and ask volunteers to show how the new image of Bernard on his own could be altered in order to make it more positive for everyone in the family; eg add mum or dad to the image of Bernard eating dinner alone; have mum, dad and Bernard sitting together to watch TV.

End with a discussion of the work and about the importance of giving attention to other family members.

Table 3.7   Task 5: management issues

The class is not paying attention to the chosen example	As soon as pupils become distracted use 'eyes on me' and or the 'five point countdown' (p. 50) to regain focus. Ask a volunteer to remind the class how the audience should behave. Identify pupils to bring into the work as figures to be sculpted
Individual responses are intentionally frivolous or to get a laugh	Accept the comments and or responses as if they were serious. Ask the pupil to justify the comment and how it contributes to the work. Making fun of others is always unacceptable and must be addressed immediately
No one responds with ideas about how to change the monster into Bernard	Volunteer yourself as a model and ask the class to 'direct' you. Guide the work through questions: 'Am I sitting?' 'Standing?'
Pupils interrupt each other, or make fun of each other during the discussion	Stop the drama and return to the classroom. Have the discussion there followed by target-setting for behaviour in drama. Return to the contract if necessary and adjust wording if appropriate

4

Beginning with story

This chapter:

o examines ways in which stories can be used as a starting point for drama work;
o considers the learning power of story in the primary years, and how traditional stories can be used as a comfortable starting point for drama;
o gives advice on selecting stories and selecting different ways of starting a story drama based on needs identification;
o looks at ways in which a story can be used and accessed at different stages in the primary years;
o explores how stories can be used to make connections across the curriculum.

The learning power of story

In earlier chapters we argued that drama in primary schools combines two powerful learning resources – story plus role play. While there may be stories of all kinds without role play, there can be no role play without a story. It is the 'bringing alive' of stories through role play, and other drama techniques and conventions, that enables important social learning to take place. In this chapter, we focus on stories as the heart of drama and also of human learning while, in Chapter 5, we turn to a detailed account of strategies for role play and using dramatic conventions.

There are a number of reasons why story is important in a school. In a profound sense we are the stories that we tell about ourselves and others; we are also shaped by the stories that others tell to us and about us. All schools, particularly urban and diverse schools like Shenton, are meeting places for stories of all kinds which affect the way pupils see themselves, their communities and others.

Pupils bring their own stories of those they love as well as the legends, myths and assumptions that make up the cultures to which they belong.

Children from different cultures bring together different stories within the school; some will fit happily alongside each other and others will be in contradiction, speak different 'truths' about the world or delimit and reinforce the differences between individuals and cultures. These stories will be personal, cultural and religious. This confluence of stories in a diverse school reminds us that we construct the world through stories, and that we do this differently – there is no one story or one truth.

A school adds to this whirlpool of storying, by introducing new stories which may be representative of what is a 'host' culture for many children – not their own culture but the culture that they will need to share in and to which they must shape themselves. Of course, the host culture is always in flux because it is constantly renewed, revisioned and reshaped by new cultural influences. Schools seek to include a diverse range of cultural stories in the curriculum, thereby giving value and recognition to the rich variety of our culture.

The primary curriculum is also built on stories of one sort or another. The history curriculum is inevitably told as stories. The pupils may focus on the facts and on the skills of historical analysis and interpretation, but what they will remember is the story of the Romans in Britain, for instance, or Florence Nightingale with her lamp. We add to these in order to recognise those whose stories tend not to be heard in history, telling the story of Mary Seacole alongside that of Florence Nightingale for example. We tell the stories of women and children at war, not just those of warriors and kings. Our stories represent injustices done, as well as 'glorifying' conquests and achievements. The stories of slavery are as important as stories of discovery and adventure.

We use stories in other subjects too. Story is at the heart of literacy and English, where children use it both to develop their skills as readers and writers, and to extend their worlds through imagination and discussion of the themes and ideas in what they read and respond to. Science often uses stories as a means of ordering scientific knowledge – we tell the story of the seasons, of frogs and plants, of the cosmos. In geography, we tell stories about how other people live – the nomads of the desert, the Inuits of the frozen north – and how their environments shape their life stories. We may use stories in maths to help pupils put 'pure' mathematical thinking into real-world contexts: 'if you had 75 pence to spend in the shop . . .'

Stories are primary acts of mind – they are the way that we think, remember, explain, communicate experience, and dream. It is natural that they should have a central place in any form of human learning, particularly in the primary years. Whereas adults differentiate their thoughts with specialised kinds of discourse, such as narrative, generalisation and theory, children must make narrative do for all. Children speak almost entirely through stories – real or invented – and they comprehend what others say through story.

Features of story

For our purposes there are some particular features of story upon which we want to concentrate. These are particularly important to our view of drama as a school improvement strategy enhancing the quality of learning and of life within a school.

o Stories engage our emotions as well as our intellects, so learning through story combines cognitive and affective dimensions of learning. We think and make meaning as we process the story, and we feel as we respond to the story. The 'feelings' aroused by a story may be a powerful motive either for children to change the story or to learn more about the context of the story in their subject learning.
o Stories arouse curiosity about what will happen and why; about causes and effects; about why people behave as they do and the moral justification for what happens to them. The twists and turns of stories can also surprise us, even shock us, causing us to think again about what we expected to happen. Stories naturally encourage a questioning and ethical problem-solving approach to learning, in keeping with the pedagogical framework outlined in Chapter 1.
o Sharing stories from different cultures and beliefs, and having the opportunity to discuss responses socially, is an important means of community building – of adding to the community's resources. Stories can be told to heal, to comfort, to disturb prejudices, to amuse, and to address issues such as racism and bullying in the community. We cannot think of an active community without thinking of the important role of story in nurturing, sustaining and explaining that sense of a living community. Whatever our differences, the universal form of story provides a common unity for sharing different experiences of the world. When we share stories from other cultures through discussion and experiencing the story as drama, it becomes 'our' story – part of our shared classroom culture.
o Story is a particularly effective learning medium because it is inclusive of a wide range of abilities as well as a wide range of cultural heritages. Children respond to the same story at different levels of understanding and intellectual engagement but they can all share and feel included in the basic plot, settings and characterisations. Different people will read at different levels and read different meanings, but they can share together in this activity – just as adults and children both find pleasure in sharing a well-told picture storybook. Later in this chapter we show how the story of Noah's Ark might be used as a cross-curriculum resource across Nursery to Year 6.

○ Stories do not divorce the concepts and the facts and figures of the curriculum from the living human contexts in which they are located. Stories allow us to give a human face to learning in the sciences and humanities in particular. Stories also focus on human behaviour and human consequences, which we want to be at the heart of a learning strategy for improving the quality of life in a school.

○ Stories help us to fix ideas and meanings in a form that allows us to remember and to exchange understandings. They can be the stable bedrock that gives some permanence to our sense of who we are, the people we belong to and our evolving history; but stories are also flexible, changeable, and renewable.

○ Traditional stories can be retold to be inclusive of new cultural influences, the outcomes of stories can be changed, stories can be told from different points of view, the settings can be changed to reflect the age, ability and culture of those sharing the story. By imagining 'what if', children can discover their own power to alter the certainties of story – What if things had been different? How would that change the outcomes of the story? This is important because, if children develop the critical skills and creative skills needed to change the stories they hear and read, then they become aware that they can also change their own story. They can be more than they imagined, they have the power to change the stories that shape them, their communities and the world they will inherit.

Many of the pupils are trying to make sense of quite different explanations and representations of the world encountered at school and in the media, but also at home, in the mosque and the madrassa. Drama provides pupils with ways of reconstructing and exploring for themselves the human experience that is represented in any story or other form of representation. This process of dramatising the experiences within stories from different points of view causes pupils to become more conscious of 'voice' and encourages critical thinking.

In a very concrete and physical way pupils can, through their drama-making, ask questions such as:

○ Who is telling the story?
○ To whom are they telling it?
○ What form does the story take?
○ What is emphasised/made invisible?
○ How else could the story be told?
○ What is the *real* story being told?

Traditional stories as a starting point for drama

As Smita, the literacy co-ordinator suggests, traditional stories make an excellent starting point for drama. They provide simple plots, context and characters for pupils to work with.

I found that traditional tales were a great way to start drama, particularly when I was new to drama and wasn't always sure about my approach. I found that as stories like *Red Riding Hood*, *Goldilocks and the Three Bears* and *Cinderella* were familiar to the children with likeable characters and a simple storyline to follow, the children were easily able to get into role, create still images, and thought track the characters. The children in my class always wanted to be the key character, particularly during hot seating and especially if props were being used.

Later, as my confidence grew, I was able to transfer the skills I had learnt through teaching drama using traditional stories to other stories I was using in literacy such as *Farmer Duck*, *The Fisherman and his Wife*, etc. Eventually I was able to use historical stories too – the Gunpowder Plot, Florence Nightingale.

Stories also introduce important moral and social themes that are relevant for the development of pupils' critical thinking skills and moral imagination in drama. These themes are the important areas of learning. Children engage first with the characters and plot of the story, but this initial engagement should lead to deeper thinking about the personal and social significance of the themes of the story.

Teachers across a year group could usefully consider which personal and social themes can be accessed through the stories, which are used in their year. Identifying the themes allows for connections to be made with other curriculum subjects and personal and social learning objectives. Children can develop characters, plots and settings through various forms of art and writing, but the ideas in a story can also be connected to concepts like 'danger', which can be explored thematically rather than tied to the particular story. We give an example of this kind of mapping in Table 4.1.

Table 4.1 Identifying the themes

Year	Story	Themes
1	Little Red Riding Hood	Growing up, danger, strangers, family responsibility
2	Goldilocks	Honesty, forgiveness, property, ownership
3	The Selfish Giant	Difference, tolerance, social responsibility
4	Hansel and Gretel	Loss and separation, family responsibility
5	Sleeping Beauty	Protection, parental responsibilities, special needs
6	King Lear	Family, loyalty, pride

When working in drama with traditional or familiar stories, children can:

o explore the issues within the story before meeting the text;
o enact scenes in the original text;
o explore the issues within the story before meeting the text;

○ take on roles from the text and be questioned about motives and intentions;
○ use space and objects (including costume) in a variety of ways to represent meanings in the text;
○ create 'missing' scenes or moments that are suggested but not fleshed out in the original text;
○ explore how to use gesture to convey 'subtext';
○ script or improvise alternative scenes or endings;
○ extend the story back in time or forward to an imagined future;
○ add or expand minor characters and their lives and involvement;
○ demonstrate to each other that there can be a variety of 'possibles' when it comes to the interpretation and representation of meanings.

Exploring the issues

Before working on *Little Red Riding Hood* (LRRH), the class could make *still images* to represent 'mother and daughter', 'looking after grandparents', 'things that scare us'. Or they could work on creating environments through drawing or making images of the 'dark, dark woods', discussing what might really be found there and what we might imagine is there.

Enacting scenes

As the teacher narrates the story of LRRH, the class act it out through mime. Volunteers or selected pupils have to physically show everything that the teacher narrates, this will include inanimate objects like the 'cottage' and the 'forest' as well as the characters. In pairs, pupils can improvise the dialogue between LRRH and her mother before she goes to visit grandmother, or between LRRH and the wolf.

Roles, motives and intentions

The teacher can take on the role of the mother and be questioned by the children about why she lets LRRH go into the dangers of the woods. This *hot seating* exercise could involve the pupils in-role as the police questioning the mother after she reports her daughter is missing, or as villagers who wonder whether she is a good mother. A child could be hot seated as LRRH just after she meets the wolf to find out what she might be thinking or feeling at that moment.

Use of space and objects

The story could be introduced through objects (including costume) – a basket, a red cloak, an old lantern – all used to help pupils remember and tell the story. In groups, pupils make an image from the story using one of these objects to make a class 'story board' of their images in sequence.

Creating 'missing' scenes or moments

The class are asked to think about LRRH's 'world' – where and how she lives. They make images/scenes to show life in her village and also to explore why the mother and daughter live alone – what happened to her father. The class make images of when they might most miss having a 'father' to support them.

Use of gesture

Pupils can explore the differences between what a character in the story might say and how they present themselves to others and what they might really be thinking and feeling on the inside. Class members could model two volunteers as images of the mother and daughter waving to each other as LRRH sets off into the woods. Pupils discuss what each character wants the other to think: 'I want her to feel safe and confident', 'I want her to know I'm a big girl and can look after myself'. They can also discuss what 'inner speech' and 'inner body image' might be going on: 'I wish I didn't have to make her go', 'Where is my father?'

Alternative scenes or endings

Pupils could improvise a 'trial' of the wolf who has only been injured by the woodcutter, with the teacher in the role of judge. Should he be put to death? Who will defend him and on what grounds? Pupils can improvise a discussion between all the main characters about how they will live now. Should Grandma move in? Are there reasons why she can't?

Extending the story back or forwards

As a form of reflection on the story, the class could make a 'photo album' of images of LRRH's future, based on shared questions about what will happen next – will Grandma move in? Will they see the woodcutter again? Will LRRH be too scared to go out again? What sort of a mother will LRRH become?

Adding or expanding minor characters

The teacher can introduce new characters to deepen the story – in a version we did we added the character of a landlord who tries to persuade Mrs Hood to let her daughter come and be his own daughter because Mrs Hood can't look after her on her own. The landlord offers to give LRRH an education and riches; what will Mrs Hood and LRRH decide? Pupils could explore the character of the woodcutter: why does he live alone in the woods? What does he know about the dangers of the woods?

Demonstrating the variety of 'possibles'

The teacher could use a simple story game in which teams of four take it in turns to retell the story. This gives children a chance to demonstrate to each other that there can be a variety of 'possibles' when it comes to the interpretation and representation of meanings. The teacher beats a drum to signal when the story should pass to the next storyteller. The game involves pupils telling the story from different perspectives, for example:

○ as Mrs Hood explaining to her neighbours what happened to her daughter;
○ as the woodcutter boasting in the village about his rescue of LRRH;
○ as the wolf, who narrowly escaped, telling his wolf family what happened;
○ as LRRH telling her own children her story as a warning about the dangers of going into the woods alone.

Different groups will respond to this task in a variety of ways.

Stories in drama as a stimulus for talk and writing:

Stories used in drama will also provide a context both for a wide range of talk registers and writing in a variety of styles and genres. Because both the story and the drama are representations of actual living, they can include the production and use of the full range of human communications in speech and writing. Writing and speaking and listening in context provides a real sense of authenticity and purpose. This is particularly important in terms of introducing non-fictional genres of writing which are demanded by the story or dramatic context.

When planning drama together, staff look to introduce these talk and writing opportunities either as part of the drama – ie used in the drama as scripts or props that develop the story – or as follow-up work in the classroom or literacy hour.

The range of talk functions in drama may include:

○ conversations, giving advice, persuasion, summarising, narrating, giving instructions;
○ expressing feelings, reflecting on actions;
○ planning, proposing.

The range of writing in drama may include:

○ notes, messages, recipes, instructions, memos, text messages, emails;
○ letters, diaries, witness statements, chronicle, archives;
○ official reports, laws of the land, job descriptions, technical details, scientific reports, church records (births, deaths, Christenings);

o writing in-role – diaries, letters, poems, journals, monologues;
o dramatic writing – scripts, scenes, stage directions.

Strategies for selecting stories

Not every traditional story or picture story book will work for drama. The best stories are those that involve social groups, rather than individual characters, who are facing real problems or dilemmas so that children can become the members of the social group and face the problems for them. Stories with strong social, moral or ethical themes are also more useful than pure fantasies; stories that focus on the social world rather than the internal psychology of characters also work better.

Indicators for choosing texts

Staff developed the following criteria and indicators for choosing drama-friendly texts.

Character

Look for *interesting characters* in the text that:

o challenge stereotypes;
o stimulate discussion;
o enable pupils to draw upon their own experiences;
o encourage pupils to experience new ways of seeing;
o experience both failure and success/demonstrate both strengths and weaknesses.

Setting

Consider the *setting* of the text in order to:

o stretch pupils' imaginations;
o encourage fantasy;
o explore historical and other 'factual' contexts;
o introduce different places from around the world;
o sustain interest;
o improve concentration;
o add value to the work;
o encourage active participation in physically creating or imagining the context.

Plot

Look for texts with strong *recurring themes*:

o eg *Into the Forest* by Anthony Browne.

Seek out texts that offer a chance for *action/movement*:

o eg *The Wizard Punchkin* (a folk tale from India) by Joanna Troughton.

Select texts that will help to *extend* and *challenge your pupil's existing vocabulary*:

o eg Shakespeare.

Select texts from *a variety of genres*, eg:

o History – *Rose Blanche* by Roberto Innocenti;
o Comedy – *Bill's New Frock* by Jacqueline Wilson;
o Myth and Legend – *Beowulf* by Kevin Crossley-Holland;
o Adventure – *The Firework-Maker's Daughter* by Philip Pullman.

Select texts *from around the world* in order to:

o introduce writing from other cultures (eg *Seasons of Splendour* by Madhur Jaffrey);
o explore writers that reflect your pupils' cultural heritage (eg *We are Britain* by Benjamin Zephaniah);
o acknowledge and value difference (eg *Life Doesn't Frighten Me at All* by Maya Angelou);
o enable your pupils to appreciate different people's perspectives (eg *Changes* by Anthony Browne).

Seek out texts that make valuable *cross-curricular links* and encourage an *integrated approach to the curriculum* (see Noah's Ark, pp. 78–85).

Story boxes and environments for story making

In addition to selecting key texts as starting points for drama work, staff also developed other story resources for each year. These included boxes and bags of objects which could be used to develop story-lines through role play or discussion. Not only do these resources act as visual and kinaesthetic stimuli for the pupils, teachers who come new to the school will be able to draw upon tried and tested resources which can be used creatively to develop engagement and interest in the story, topic or issue.

Introducing a story or a theme with a collection of simple but purposeful objects can prompt immediate discussion as well as acting as a 'hook' to engage learners in the work (see Table 4.2). What were the items used for? How are they connected? Who might they belong to and what are we going to do with them?

The objects might be used to help pupils to make up their own stories, or they might be used by a character introduced through 'Teacher-in-role' or role play. (See the example of objects used to begin a drama about Florence Nightingale on p. 69.)

Table 4.2   Story or topic boxes/bags

Little Red Riding Hood	The Victorians	At the seaside
○ A basket/tea-towel	○ Some old pictures/postcards,	○ A bucket
○ Some sweets/biscuits	or a photograph of a family	○ A spade
○ A red cape	○ A letter	○ A postcard
○ A shawl	○ A wash board	○ A net
○ Directions	○ A tin bath	○ Sand, shells and
○ A picture of a forest	○ An ice cream wrapper	seaweed

The use of 'role play' environments is not limited to the Early Years. Pupils of all ages are given the opportunity to explore and experiment in 'environments', which have been carefully constructed to stimulate responses, ideas and discussion connected to unfamiliar times, places or situations. Environments can be constructed with guided learning in mind, ie to help establish context or introduce new vocabulary or simply as spaces in which pupils are given the opportunity to 'play' independently or in small groups.

Sometimes a drama might begin with entry into a previously unseen environment. On other occasions the environment might have been created by the pupils during an art lesson or project. Once completed, theatrical lighting and or sound might also be used to help build the atmosphere. In some instances roles might be introduced, suggested or adopted according to the intention of the environment. 'Teacher-in-role' (see pp. 94–101) is an effective way to bring the environment to life or as the children become more confident they themselves might volunteer to invent characters of their own or borrow from familiar stories.

Environments are also an effective multi-sensory approach to learning. If you are not stimulated by touch – the bark underfoot or the sand running through your fingers – then it might be colours which draw you in – the sparkling azure and emerald of the sea or the light which spotlights a copy of *The Big Issue* next to an old sleeping bag. It might be the sounds which emerge from the woods – bells tied to seaweed strips or the rustle of newspaper underfoot. Or for many the engagement is realised through tension that mounts from the unfamiliar – the shadow that appears from behind the tree, or the body which emerges from beneath the pile of cardboard boxes.

Table 4.3   Environments

A Forest	Underwater Environment	The Homeless
Role – a woodcutter	**Role – a merman/maid**	**Role – someone homeless**
○ Tree bark	○ Seaweed	○ Piles of newspaper
○ Leaves	○ Fish	○ Cardboard boxes
○ Flowers	○ Blue lengths of material	○ A blanket
○ Litter	○ White/green/blue netting/	○ Empty food packets
○ A log to sit on	ribbon to hang things from	○ A photograph
○ Lengths of different textured	○ Shells	○ A picture of a dog
material (green/brown, etc)	○ Sand	○ Some old clothes
		○ Copy of *The Big Issue*

Different ways of starting story dramas

Choosing a good story for drama work is an important step forward, but there is still the tricky question as to how to actually begin the drama in ways that will give confidence and motivation to pupils while ensuring from the teacher's point of view that the work is thoughtful, purposeful and controlled.

Smita, the literacy co-ordinator, reminds us that books are not the only starting point for story and drama explorations in the curriculum:

> I used the following objects to develop a drama based on Florence Nightingale: poster of army hospital scene; lantern; bandages.

> The poster was used as a stimulus to generate words and phrases about the state of army hospitals. It led to some still images being created of wounded soldiers in appalling hospital conditions. This is where the bandages were used to heighten the soldiers' wounds and injuries. This then led to a thought-tracking activity where children empathised with the wounded soldier. The lantern was used during a hot seating activity where a child in-role introduced herself as Florence Nightingale, expressed her thoughts about the conditions of hospitals and how she uses her lantern to bring some light to the injured and then proceeded to answer questions from other children.

Objects, or props, have a special value in drama. They are read as having a symbolic importance – so bandages will symbolise war and conflict, death and injury in this Crimean War context. The lantern will symbolise healing, concern for the suffering, bringing 'light' into the awful conditions suffered by the injured. By using these objects in context, the pupils are engaged in thinking beyond the facts of the Florence Nightingale story. The objects also help children to engage at a feeling level with the remote events of the Crimean War.

The most common questions that have arisen are 'How do I start the drama?' or, 'I know what I want to teach, but how and where do I begin?' In teaching any subject, it is important to begin by considering the particular needs of the pupils.

This might include addressing the social health of the class (their ability to concentrate, to work together, to work independently, levels of confidence and self-esteem, as well as their ability to respond positively to each other). It is also important to consider your own and your pupils' experience of drama work, as well as their levels of creative and imaginative energy. Teachers will also want to consider what other learning and teaching activities are taking place that day, and how the drama work might build on or affect this.

In the section below we chose to focus on a number of different ways of beginning drama work on *Sleeping Beauty*. Staff identify the benefits of each activity based on their experiences of drama so far.

Possible reasons for starting the drama with a 'thought-shower'

o The pupils may be new to drama.
o The technique gives the teacher a chance to check pupils' knowledge of subject matter and reinforce their vocabulary.
o A thought-shower can generate discussion in pairs, in small- or in whole-group settings (those that are less confident feel more able to speak in small group settings).

Benefits for pupils

1 This approach helps pupils with EAL and/or low self-esteem, because pupils are required to share their ideas.
2 It helps to increase understanding of a subject by using new vocabulary, perhaps useful for the most able.
3 This approach helps pupils with limited life experience, by extending what they already know through social learning from others.

Example 1

Sit the class down in a circle with a large piece of sugar paper in front of you. In the middle of the sugar paper is the title *Sleeping Beauty*. Ask pupils what words, images, emotions, characters, etc they associate with the title.

Possible reasons for starting the drama with a game

A game can be used to:

o energise the class;
o calm or focus the class;
o introduce the theme;
o reinforce understanding of 'rule-bound' activity;
o develop team-building/turn-taking skills.

Benefits for pupils

1 Games encourage active participation from everyone.
2 They help to refocus pupils with behavioural problems.
3 Games can be familiar to pupils and provide a safe experience through rules and taking turns.

Example 2

Players spread out in the room and close their eyes. The teacher touches one player on the shoulder. This child now becomes the 'thirteenth fairy'. On the word from the teacher, the players begin to walk slowly through the space, keeping their eyes closed at all times. The aim is to meet as many people as possible, hopefully avoiding the thirteenth fairy. To meet someone the child reaches out and takes them by the arm and asks the question 'thirteenth fairy?', to which they will receive the reply 'thirteenth fairy!'. At this point they move on and try to meet someone else. Meanwhile the 'thirteenth fairy' too is moving through the space with his or her eyes closed and meeting people, but saying nothing through the game. So on asking 'thirteenth fairy?', if the players hear nothing, they ask it another time, 'thirteenth fairy?' just to make sure. If they hear no reply then they have met and touched the thirteenth fairy and must fall asleep for a hundred years before retiring to the side of the room. The game concludes when all the players have been caught.

Possible reasons for starting the drama with an image

An image can do the following:

o offer a visual 'way in' to the subject matter;
o enable pupils to feel a sense of ownership over the material, including what is known, what is imagined, and so on;
o make a simple 'text' to illustrate first ideas about the story or its themes, as children use their bodies, space and simple props;
o use pupils' own images to begin discussion and exploration of the story's themes in particular.

Benefits for pupils

1 Using an image works to the strengths of visual and kinaesthetic learners in particular.
2 In an image, what you see is what you get. So an image provides pupils of all abilities with the opportunity to suggest an idea based upon it, or to describe the obvious features of the image as a starting point for discussion.
3 EAL pupils can engage with and be affected by the visual clues and 'atmosphere' of the image even if they don't follow some of the language used to

describe it. They can make strong physical and visual contributions to images made by the class.

4 When making their own image as a starting point, pupils can quickly make a 'text' which expresses their ideas and which can be read and discussed by other pupils.

Example 3

With the class sitting in a circle, hand out copies of two contrasting images of Sleeping Beauty – a pretty and gentle one, such as the familiar Disney image, and a different (more complex) one such as that by Dürer.

o What do we know?
  (What can we see in the picture? What is factual?)
o What do we guess?
  (What do we think or imagine might be going on in the picture?)
o What do we want to know more about?
  (What do we want to find out? What questions does the picture make us ask?)

Possible reasons for starting the drama with an object

An object:

o offers visual and tactile stimuli;
o develops and stretches the imagination;
o encourages pupils to ask questions.

Benefits for pupils

1 Starting with an object works to the strengths of the more curious and tactile pupils, who enjoy a visual/sensory experience and detective work.
2 Objects can bring life to the session and provide something concrete to stimulate imaginative responses.
3 Using and handling objects may be easier for pupils who find it difficult to get into role.

Example 4

The class sit in the circle; the teacher holds up a piece of 'unspun flax' or some other object associated with spinning wheels, and asks the pupils what the object suggests or what kind of a story this might be.

Possible reasons for starting the drama with text

An appropriately chosen text can:

○ develop literacy skills, for example by introducing new vocabulary, creating opportunities for reading, focusing on speaking and listening;
○ challenge more able pupils;
○ introduce characters and settings in a 'literary' form, crafted by a skilled writer;
○ provide clues which the pupils can pick up on in order to make deductive inferences about the story and its themes.

Benefits for pupils

1 Using a text works to the strengths of able readers and those pupils who need structure and direction to feel comfortable.
2 It recognises that some pupils enjoy working with text, accessing new vocabulary, and predicting what has happened, or will happen next.
3 Texts help pupils who have weak or limited vocabulary.

Example 5

Provide the class with a fragment of text (alternatively you could put the text onto an OHT).

> A long time ago there lived a King and a Queen who had no children, and this grieved them more than can be imagined. Every day they wished, 'If only we had a child', but the days passed and they remained childless.
>
> However, one day as the Queen was bathing in a forest pool, a little frog came out of the water and said to her, 'Your dearest wish shall soon be fulfilled. Before a year has passed you shall bring a daughter into the world.' The Queen went home and told her husband what had happened, and sure enough, the frog's words came true.

Move around the circle and ask each pupil in turn to read up until the next punctuation mark. Once the text has come to an end ask the next pupil in turn to start from the beginning again but this time read as if trying to capture the interest of the listener by developing their use of voice (varying volume, emphasis, emotional involvement and pace). As the text ends for a second time ask the next pupil to read again, but this time invite others to come into the circle as particular characters and objects are introduced (the King and Queen, the forest, the pool, the frog, etc) and act the story out.

Possible reasons for starting the drama with a dilemma

A dilemma will enable you to:

○ engage the class in the real dilemmas in which the characters find themselves, and which they must resolve;

○ offer pupils responsibility for deciding which is the best course of action to take;
○ develop skills in problem-solving which require moral and ethical judgements to be made;
○ explore the morality of a given situation.

Benefits for pupils

1 The dilemma encourages lively debate about moral choices – what is the right thing to do?
2 The discussion of the dilemma and its personal consequences for character may help pupils who have little empathy for others.
3 Working through the dilemma help pupils to safely explore the moral and other consequences of particular actions.

Example 6

Groups of four or five pupils become 'families' of spinners and weavers. Working with wool is how they earn their living. In their groups, the 'actors' discuss what their work might involve, how hard it is, how dangerous, etc. Remind the class, for example, that 'spinning' at night would be done by candlelight. Using mime or still images each family group shows a day in the life of a spinner's family. This may be accompanied by writing in-role or diary entries, for example.

Bring the class back together in a circle. 'Teacher-in-role' as King explains that in order to protect his daughter all spinning wheels in the Kingdom will be destroyed immediately. They are told to go to their homes and bring back their spinning wheels.

Out of role, send pupils back into their original 'family' groups to discuss whether or not they are prepared to hand over their only means of earning a living.

Possible reasons for starting the drama with 'Teacher-in-role' (see Chapter 5, pp. 94–101)

Using the techniques of 'Teacher-in-role' can help the teacher to:

○ grab pupils' attention;
○ develop listening skills;
○ reinforce meaning with body language and other visual clues;
○ manage difficult behaviour through 'role';
○ model language and physical expression appropriate to character and situation.

Benefits for pupils

1 Interacting as themselves with the teacher in-role is a good way of starting for those pupils reluctant to participate in-role.

2 It provides a clear model of the appropriate language and behaviour expected from pupils when they enter into role themselves.

3 It motivates those pupils who may have a low level of cultural understanding regarding the material.

4 The teacher can target pupils and differentiate his or her responses to ensure that there is inclusion and opportunities for everyone to be involved.

5 It can help more able children to develop and elaborate their thoughts to help their writing. It increases their expectations and provides a good model of working 'in-role', ie the teacher's use of voice, expression and movement.

Example 7

The class have been working as the 'good fairies' that have been invited to the Christening of the new royal baby. They draw gifts for the child, and the teacher welcomes them to the Christening in-role as King. The pairs present their gifts two by two, placing them in the baby's crib. Then the 'King' seeks their advice on how to be a good father and how best to look after his daughter. The King also tells the story of the twelve golden plates and explains, in-role, to the 'good fairies' that he hasn't invited the 'fairy of the thorns' because he didn't have enough plates and anyway she is so old and grumpy!

Possible reasons for starting the drama with sound

Sound can:

o provoke imaginative engagement with the 'feel' of the sound;
o develop pupils' aural skills;
o encourage pupils to develop alternative ways of making and communicating meaning;
o help increase attention through creating atmosphere.

Benefits for pupils

1 Sound works to the strengths of aural learners and those with musical intelligence.

2 It can stimulate and motivate those pupils who find it hard to maintain concentration.

3 It provides a strong sense of atmosphere and suspense for those who need to be engaged at a feeling level.

Example 8

With the class sat in the circle ask them to thought-shower all that they know about the story of *Sleeping Beauty*. Their responses might include aspects of the environment, such as the castle, the courtyard, the celebratory party, etc. It might include the characters, the King, the Queen, the bad fairy, the Prince, etc. Or it might include aspects of the story: the cutting down of the thorny briar, the men who lost their lives doing this, the long sleep, etc. When you have explored these themes, divide the class into groups to develop a soundtrack for different parts of the story, as shown in Table 4.4.

Table 4.4   Themes for a soundtrack, by group

Group 1	The palace
Group 2	The thorny briar and those who tried to penetrate it
Group 3	The long sleep
Group 4	The secret tower
Group 5	The castle awakes

After rehearsing, everyone is asked to find a space by themselves in the room. A volunteer is invited to move around the room slowly. As they move near to someone that person must begin their soundtrack; as they move away from them, the sounds must stop. Inviting others to walk in different spaces at the same time could develop this further. Ask the group to consider what effect this has on them and their understanding of the story.

Possible reasons for starting the drama with movement

Movement allows pupils to:

○ develop the ability to communicate physically;
○ offer alternative ways of expressing themselves emotionally and intellectually;
○ create instant and independent responses through movement;
○ develop negotiation skills in time and space.

Benefits for pupils

1 Using movement works to the strengths of those pupils who have strong spatial awareness and who best express themselves physically.
2 It provides a form of differentiation for pupils who find language difficult as they have the opportunity to express themselves through movement and gesture.
3 It can show children appropriate use of physical movement.
4 It allows negotiation of the more symbolic uses of movement as dance can be challenging and rewarding for groups.
5 It stimulates active learners, children who prefer this style of learning to sitting down and writing.

Example 9

Ask pupils to find a space in the room. Explain to the pupils that they will be asked to take a walk around the room 'as if' exploring the inside of a 'Kingdom'. At various intervals you will call out various phrases that will signal pupils to make either individual or collective images. Examples could include:

o single image prompts: Princess, Prince, King, Queen, good fairy, bad fairy, frog;
o group image prompts: a castle, a secret tower, a forest of thorns, a celebration.

(NB: Indicate to pupils the number of pupils needed for group images.)

Possible reasons for starting the drama with an environment

Starting with an environment can:

o encourage pupils to respond independently;
o focus on kinaesthetic, visual and aural learners;
o develop opportunities for imaginative play;
o introduce and develop pupils' understanding of mood and atmosphere.

Benefits for pupils

1 Starting with an environment allows kinaesthetic, visual and aural learners to combine their strengths to create a 'set' for the story based on their imaginings of what a place in the story would be like to the senses, including smell, touch, climate, etc.
2 It provides a three-dimensional model of a story setting for those children with limited cultural experiences of different environments (woods, clinics, caves, etc).
3 Environments build on the familiarity of 'play spaces' in the foundation years and can help to open up imagination and the opportunity for creative thinking.

This task needs some organisation and preparation before the lesson begins and can be explored at varying degrees of complexity and artistry. An activity like this is designed to provide pupils with a sensory experience of the 'story environment'. To help create this environment, you might choose to use (depending upon time and availability) stage lights, music, sound effects, objects, props, material hanging, projected images and so on, to help create the central mood or atmosphere within the story.

Example 10

Using simple props including bamboo canes and saris, along with whatever lighting and other technology is available, pupils create one or more of the environments suggested in the story: the secret tower where the girl pricks her finger on the spinning wheel; the castle; the 'bad fairy's' cave where she makes her spells and potions.

Alternatively, the class can make themselves into the tangled forest of briars that engulfs the castle. They begin in small groups and then, accompanied by music, they all gather together into one tangled forest, which is thick and dense and thorny!

In Chapter 5 we turn our attention to working in-role and using the full range of dramatic techniques and conventions to initiate, develop and reflect on story-based dramas. The last section of this chapter, however, looks at how a story can be adapted for use with different age groups and across the curriculum.

Story drama across the years and across the curriculum

In this final section we use the story of *Noah's Ark* to demonstrate how the same traditional story might be used with different age groups and to inform the teaching of a range of subjects. This work is based on a training and staff development exercise. The staff agreed to work on this story with all the year groups as the basis for a staff meeting where they could share their experiences, discuss common concerns, identify the learning potential of drama in different years and begin to consider what progression in drama might look like. Staff also agreed to map out curriculum connections with the story in their year.

This work has two uses here. Firstly, to model how story drama might progress from one year to the next and how a story can be used as a matrix to help pupils make connections between subjects. Secondly, as a model for planning a similar staff development initiative either based on this story or another chosen by staff.

Noah's Ark: Sequence of drama tasks for Nursery class children

Task 1: Huggy

Ask pupils to find a space and on the sound of the drum move slowly in different directions around the room. When the teacher calls 'Huggy Three' pupils must get into a group of three and form a group hug. The game continues calling different numbers.

This game could be linked to the rhyme 'The Animals Went in Two by Two'. The class must keep moving until the teacher calls 'the animals went in two by two', or 'three by three', etc. As the teacher calls the number of animals together, the pupils must respond by repeating the line as they find a partner or group.

The animals went in two by two, hurrah! hurrah!

Task 2: God's order

Sit the class back in a circle. Explain that they are going to hear a story about a man and his family who were ordered by their God to make a great big wooden boat. Everyone in the class is to hold hands and to stretch out in the shape of a boat with round sides and two points at each end. The teacher goes on to describe the boat in more detail while the children stand and listen:

o it was made from wood;
o there was cabin for the family on the top deck;
o shelter for the animals below deck;
o round windows in the body of the Ark for the animals to look out from, etc.

The teacher may also describe how the boat must be strong enough to sail the open seas and get the class to work together in their boat shape to show how the boat will go up and down in the waves, rock from side to side in the storms, float in the still waters when there is no wind.

Task 3: Building the Ark

Ask the class what activities Noah and his family would have had to do in order to make the Ark. Make a list of three or four activities such as chopping down trees, sawing wood or hammering nails. Ask someone in the group to model each activity with the rest of the group copying the action. Divide the class into activity groups to mime their work while 'Teacher-in-role' Noah goes around offering encouragement, commenting on their work, chatting to the workers, etc.

Task 4: The animals board the Ark two by two

Everyone should help to make the shape of the boat again, this time using chairs or benches for its outline. Now explain that Noah was ordered to take two of every animal in the world. Ask the class to think of what animals might be taken on board. Make a list. Decide how each of the animals on the list might be represented: the elephant with a swinging trunk; the monkey with swaying arms; the giraffe with a stretched out neck, etc.

Then explain that the animals are going to board the Ark in pairs. The class line up in pairs at one end of the boat. The teacher narrates which animals board first and how they move – as the teacher narrates the pupils move on board the Ark and sit huddled in the group. Once all the animals are on board the teacher narrates the beginning of the rainstorm (using a rain stick) and the 'animals' respond appropriately. The class can now reflect on their work and the story.

Noah's Ark: Sequence of drama tasks for children in Years 1 and 2

Warm up game: Noah in charge

Explain that each 'command' that Noah gives has an action which pupils must respond to. The person who responds the slowest or carries out an incorrect action must sit out from the game. The game continues until there are one or two individuals remaining or until it's time to move on to the next activity.

(NB: *You could develop the game by adding the condition that they must only move if 'Noah says animal overboard'. If someone moves without Noah having said so they are out.*)

Table 4.5 Commands and responses for warm-up

Commands:	Activities:
Port	Run to the left of the space
Starboard	Run to the right of the space
Noah is coming	Hold hands with your partner
Scrub the decks	Get on your hands and knees and scrub the deck
Animal overboard	Mime swimming to rescue it
Waves ahead	Sway from side to side
Heatwave	Lie on back and sunbathe

Task 1: Presenting Noah

Explain that you are going to go into role as Noah.

(NB: *Select a prop or item of costume to indicate that you are going into role, for example, a headscarf or staff. When you remove or put down the costume or prop, you will come out of role.*)

'Teacher-in-role' Noah sits with his head in his hands. He seems very worried. He mutters to himself, then he looks out into the valley and shakes his head. For example:

> 'Why do they hate each other so much? Why must they hurt each other with words that are so unkind? What has become of this beautiful world? Look at the litter! Our view is spoilt. Stealing from those who have little. Taking what is not theirs. I want a better world for my children, for my boys, Shem, Ham and Japeth.'

Ask the pupils to comment on what they have heard. Ask them why Noah is so upset. What has he seen to make him feel this way?

Task 2: Life in the valley

Explain that the class is going to create a *collective image* of life in the valley. Using a large piece of sugar paper, make a note of the things that Noah might have seen in the valley. Then using the list for reference ask for two volunteers to come into the circle to create an image from the list. Those pupils watching could act as directors and help *sculpt* the image to help communicate their meaning with effect.

Once pupils feel comfortable with what they are expected to do invite them one at a time to come into the circle and use each other to create the *collective image*, building upon each others' ideas.

(NB: You might want to play some music as the pupils get into position.)

Once the image is complete the teacher begins to narrate over what has been created, drawing attention to particular aspects of the image and what they are trying to communicate: 'In the valley, I can see that there is a lot of conflict, some people seem to be very greedy and don't want to share what they have', etc.

Ask the class to bring their image to life for a brief moment, while taking the time to look around at what they have created collectively. Ask if there is a character or an aspect of the image that they are particularly interested in. Then ask everyone to gather round the selected work.

Task 3: What were they thinking?

Pupils observing are invited to *thought-track* any one of the characters in the chosen image. Model if appropriate. Invite pupils to comment on how they feel about what they have heard.

Task 4: Finger puppets

Pupils use finger puppets of animals made earlier in the classroom. In pairs pupils create *conversations* that the animals might have together before boarding the Ark. For example, the monkey might be worried about having no trees to swing from, the giraffe about having no leaves to eat, and the leopard about having nowhere to race around, etc. Share some of the conversations with the rest of the class, with the teacher clicking fingers over a pair to stop or start their conversation.

Noah's Ark: Sequence of drama tasks for children in Years 3 and 4

Task 1: A letter from God

An envelope is placed in the middle of the circle. Invite one person to go into the circle, as Noah, open the envelope and read its content to the rest of the group.

Dear Noah

I have come to a decision. I cannot watch the world be destroyed any longer by humans. I have decided to send a great flood to wash away all that is wrong with the world. You must build a boat big enough for your wife, your sons and their wives, a pair of every animal in the world, and food enough to feed them for a very long time. Then wait for the waters to rise.

Yours in trust

God

Ask the pupils to consider what action Noah needs to take in order to prepare for the flood. Collectively the group compile a list to help Noah, putting tasks in order of priority.

Task 2: Building the Ark

Groups of three, four or five pupils are asked to create a still image to show the type of activities and/or jobs that will need to be completed before the floods come. Activities could include: chopping wood, hammering, selecting the animals, preparing food, informing the family and neighbours.

Task 3: Mrs Noah the doubter

Explain to the group that persuading Mrs Noah about events to come is perhaps going to be Noah's greatest challenge. In groups of four or five, pupils must plan how they are going to inform Mrs Noah from the following perspectives:

1 The whole class, or volunteers in-role, takes on the *collective role* of Noah, having to break the news to the 'Teacher-in-role' as a doubting and hard-to-convince Mrs Noah about what he has been asked to do.
2 The whole class, or volunteers in-role, as the sons of Noah asking their mother to help build the Ark; she can't see the point and thinks they are all wasting their time.
3 The whole class, or volunteers, confront Mrs Noah about rumours surrounding the flood and ask if they will be saved on the Ark as well. Mrs Noah dismisses their concerns and assures them there is 'no way' she will be getting on board.
4 Once the rain clouds begin to gather, the whole class, or volunteers, break the news that she cannot bring her friends.
5 The whole class in the role of the family – including Noah – try to persuade Mrs Noah to board the Ark as it begins to rain. It is only when she is standing up to her waist in rainwater that she gives in!

(NB: Remind the group that they must plan out their ideas together as you, in-role, as Mrs Noah will become part of the improvised scene, interacting and working with the other characters.)

Task 4: The animals came in two by two

Divide the class into pairs. Explain that together they must decide what animal pair they are going to be. They must create a short story which is to be presented to the audience orally, telling of an incident which happened on their way to the Ark. This might have been an argument between other animals that had not been chosen or something they had seen which had upset them, such as people behaving badly in the valley.

Noah's Ark: Sequence of drama tasks for children in Years 5 and 6

Work with this age group may also include some of the activities suggested for earlier years.

Task 1: How do I choose?

'Teacher-in-role' Noah calls a family meeting and members of Noah's family (the pupils) are invited to attend. Three men have turned up from a neighbouring village, yet only two can be chosen to board the ark. Noah has a dilemma which he cannot face alone and asks his family how he can choose between them. Should he judge them on their qualities, values, beliefs or skills? Should he choose the oldest, the wisest or what?

(NB: The length of the meeting depends upon the level of debate and interest that is initiated by the pupils; it is important that a particular solution is not agreed upon at this point.)

Task 2: Then came the rains

Pupils stay in the circle and are told that the rains are coming. As a group they are going to create the *sound track* for the rainstorm.

From their seats, pupils practise making four 'rain' sounds: rubbing palms, snapping fingers, tapping knees, and pounding feet. Ask them to close their eyes. You or a pupil starts the first sound and spreads it around the circle with each person following the person next to him or her. After the first sound has travelled all around the circle, you or a pupil begins the second sound which travels in the same way and so on. Build the sounds up from silence to an intense storm.

Depending upon time you might want to experiment by layering the sounds with text. Pupils are given a handout of the text below. From this they select a sentence or word(s) which they like and feel comfortable in saying. Select one pupil to read the entire text. When the reader comes to their word/sentence then they must overlap. This continues until the text ends. Experiment with the way in which words are spoken (in fear, whispered, angrily or emphasising particular sounds as the word(s) are spoken). Once this has been practised, it could then be spoken over the sounds created earlier.

> It rained for forty days.
> It rained for forty nights.
> It rained harder than Noah had ever seen before.
> It rained so hard the streams burst their banks.
> It rained so hard the rivers burst their banks.
> It rained so hard the seas spilt over the land.
> It rained so hard the lands began to flood.
> Soon every sandy beach, every rocky path, every patch of muddy earth had disappeared beneath the water.
> And the boat began to float.
> Above the houses.
> Above the trees.
> Above the hills and mountains too.
> It floated for days and weeks and months.

Task 3: Making the headlines

Explain to the class that in order to keep themselves busy while on board the Ark, and as a lasting record of events, the family and animals produced a weekly newsheet, *Noah's Times*. Divide the class into groups of five, each of which must create a *news headline* of something which might have made the front page of the paper during their time afloat.

Once each group has created a headline these are then given out to a different group to create a *still image* to accompany the headline. After these have been shared and possibly recorded using a digital camera, ask the class to select one character from each of the images. Then ask these characters to sit in a circle of five chairs.

Pupils are then given the opportunity to *hot seat* the characters in-role as 'news reporters' in preparation for the story that will follow the headline and photograph.

Activity 4: A new beginning

Explain to the pupils that Noah's God sent the floods so that the world could begin again, free from violence and hatred. Ask them to think for a moment how they might imagine their own world differently? What would it look like? Discuss a few responses. Ask pupils to think of a statement which reflects their imagined picture of a better world or an element of it (such as 'Peace on earth'). This could be done in pairs. Move around the circle and listen to each statement in turn. Next ask the pupils to create a gesture or an action which might accompany this. Explain that you are going to play a piece of music, when this begins they must move into the circle and take up a position using their gesture, once in position they speak their statement and then freeze until every pupil is within the image.

Links between the work on *Noah's Ark* and various different areas of the curriculum can be found in Table 4.6. Further resources can be found on the publisher's website (www.fultonpublishers.co.uk).

Table 4.6 An example of keeping the curriculum connected through drama – 'Noah's Ark'

	Nursery and F1/2	1	2	3	4	5	6
Science	Create an animal alphabet using the animals found on the Ark.	*Classification:* Identify and sort animals on board the Ark.	*Materials and their properties:* Explore what materials float and sink. Decide which materials would be most suitable to build an Ark from.	*Green plants as organisms:* Experiment with what happens to seeds which are: 1. over-watered; 2. under-watered; 3. watered daily.			
English		Make a simple *picture story book* of 'Noah's Ark' using digital photographs taken from the drama work. Add captions to each image to summarise each event.	*Discuss question language:* What, where, how, why, when – use questions to 'hot seat' the 'Teacher-in-role' as Noah.	Use *visual aids* when *explaining* own design/model of an Ark.	Write a short *play script* to explore some of the arguments which might have taken place on board the Ark between Noah's family or the animals.	*Oral storytelling:* in small groups explore the story of *Noah's Ark* from different character's perspectives, eg Noah, Mrs Noah, a neighbour, etc.	Use *journalistic styles and conventions* when reporting major events which took place on board the Ark while it was at sea.
D&T	*Use soft construction kits* to make a model of the Ark.	*Sew animal outlines using templates* and make animal finger puppets to be used in the drama work.			*Sawing and Joining:* Design and build a small scale Ark from wood and card.	*Design* and *make* own instruments from recycled materials eg plastic bottles / containers etc.	
History			*Famous people and famous events:* Explore why Noah is so famous in the West. What are we to learn from him?		Identify the great floods which have happened throughout history, across different continents. What impact did these floods have on the people and how did it shape their lives?		Look at the oldest story in history 'Gilgamesh' (700 BC) and explore links with the story of Noah's Ark.

Geography	*Explore simple weather*, from dry to wet conditions / from rain to storm.	*Weather:* Effects of weather on people and their surroundings. Look at the story book *Bringing the Rain to Kapiti Plain* by Verna Aardema and Beatriz Vidal.	*A mountain environment:* The search for Noah's Ark on Mount Ararat (see www. arksearch.com).	*Weather – seasonal weather patterns and the effects on people:* What happens when the rains don't come? Look at famine in Africa.	*Influence of weather:* Coping with natural disaster, eg the flooding in Mumbai and Boscastle. Follow true story accounts of how the floods have affected people's lives.
Art	*Develop an awareness of colour/shape/ texture:* in the form of a 3D collage of the Ark.	Design and make animal masks using *powder paints* and *coloured wool*.	In *pencil* design own Ark and label the features. This design will be used in English.	Create *clay models* of the full range of animals found on board the Ark. Divide the class into pairs. Each pair is given different animals to model.	Create a landscape drawing of the Ark as the waters begin to subside and the land begins to emerge using *charcoal*.
Music	*Sing nursery rhymes and simple songs from memory:* The Animals Went in Two by Two Hurrah. Explore dynamics from loud to quiet. Use Jan Pienkowski's pop-up story book to accompany the singing.	*Listening and appraising:* Identify the feelings experience by animals on board the Ark. Identify which feelings are associated with the different musical extracts.		*Performing and composing:* Create a soundscape for the story of Noah's Ark, eg the elements – the rains beginning to the great floods.	*Sounds and inventions:* Using the poem 'The Late Passenger' by C.S. Lewis create a soundscape to accompany the poem. Use recycled instruments made in D&T. The sounds could be recorded and used to accompany the movement work in dance.

(continued)

Table 4.6 Continued

	Nursery and F1/2	1	2	3	4	5	6
PE		Explore the way in which different animals **move and interact together** (despite their differences) to music.	Use the musical extracts used above as a stimulus for creating **movements** associated with different animals and how they are feeling on board the Ark, eg trapped/threatened, etc. Pupils work with animal masks made in art.			Use extracts from the poem 'The Late Passenger' by C.S. Lewis as a stimulus for **movement work in dance**. The recording created in music could be used to accompany the work produced.	Explore Helen Ward's story 'The Boat' through **dance**. A strange man/unwanted animals/mutual fear and mistrust separating people/terrible storms/a great flood and a boat.
RE	**Creation stories:** Look at other creation stories from a variety of cultures.	**Living things:** Explore work on animal charities. RSPCA/Battersea Dogs Home, etc.		**Leaders:** Explore the qualities we admire/link to leadership, eg Jesus/Noah.		**Responsibility for the environment:** Focus on the school and community environment. What are the problems and how might they be overcome if the community worked together?	

ICT		*Communicating information using text:* Print out the questions that Noah was asked about the Ark and the great floods using writer.	Use ICT to bring written work, eg play scripts created in English, into a *published form.*	Create a *spreadsheet to display data* from a whole school survey on looking after the environment. What do staff, parents and pupils think about the environment in their community?	Create a *multimedia presentation* to reflect on work surrounding *Noah's Ark.* This might include moving or still digital images or work produced in dance, images of floods downloaded from the web, headlines and news stories created in English of major events of the Ark.
Maths	*Number:* counting animals onto the Ark. *Shapes* found on the Ark, eg round windows.	*Shape:* Use math's names for common 2/3D shapes/sort shapes/describe shape patterns found on the Ark.	*Shape:* Use the pin board/elastic board/squared paper to describe and make the shapes found on the Ark.	*Measure:* Provide the class with a scale drawing of the Ark. Pupils can work out the size of given areas, eg cabin space in cm^2.	

Other related stories and websites:

Nursery:
Text:
Noah's Ark – Lucy Cousins / Walker Books ISBN: 074455540X

Key Stage 1:
Text:
Bringing the Rain to Kapiti Plain – Verna Aardema /Macmillan ISBN: 0333351649
Noah's Ark – Jane Ray / Orchard Paperbacks ISBN: 1852139471
The Animals Went in Two by Two / Candlewick Press ISBN: 0763619914

Key Stage 2:
Text:
Once Upon a Poem (The Late Passenger by C.S.Lewis) Forward by Kevin Crossley-Holland / The Chicken House ISBN: 1904442315
Gilgamesh The Hero – Geraldine McCaughrean / Oxford University Press ISBN: 0192741861
The Boat – Helen Ward / Templar Publishings ISBN: 1840114029
Websites:
www.arksearch.com
www.talkorigins.org
www.fultonpublishers.co.uk

5

Acting to learn

This chapter:

- o looks at two key drama strategies – 'Teacher-in-role' and 'Mantle of the Expert';
- o gives advice and examples for each of these two ways of working at Nursery level, Key Stage 1 and Key Stage 2;
- o identifies reasons for choosing different dramatic conventions, and gives detailed advice (in Table 5.1) on how to work with them;
- o uses a Year 6 lesson based on *King Lear* to model how these techniques can be used to develop and deepen role play.

Our model for drama in the primary years is based on combining the learning power of story with various forms of role play which enable the children to take on the characters and situations in story 'as if' they were real for them. Role play turns the story into a living experience for children.

At the heart of all drama is the use of our natural capacity to imagine ourselves 'differently'. This imagining begins from the 'what if' – imagining ourselves in different times, places and 'shoes' and moves quickly to the 'as if' – behaving as if we were in a different time, place and role. Traditional and other stories give us the 'what if' needed for imaginative drama work to begin. Stories provide us with a context and with characters and problems that need resolving or understanding. Of course, teachers were already familiar with using stories as a regular starting point for literacy work, but drama offered a new and active dimension for learning about story and learning through stories.

Drama provides the means for pupils to enter into the story by taking on roles, rather than merely listening privately to the story. By taking on the roles of characters in stories, they are able to behave 'as if' they were inside the story, facing the same experiences, hopes, fear and problems as the story characters. Imagining ourselves differently by taking on roles is at the heart of the drama work done.

Each day we move within a range of different social situations. Children, whether in the company of their parents, teachers, elders, relatives, community or religious leaders, friends or peers have to consider what role they need to adopt, from which register and dialect to select and, increasingly, how to present themselves physically, through their facial gesture and body language when they meet, work and play with others. These factors are also important in drama.

In this chapter wc want to focus on two key strategies for role play: 'Teacher-in-role' and 'Mantle of the Expert'. In the first strategy, the teacher takes on a role in the drama in order to initiate, guide, include and develop the children's learning through role taking. In the second strategy the class are given the roles of experts who must work together to resolve a real world problem.

Learning in-role

We all have some experience of working in-role with children, particularly with younger children who will often invite us into their dramatic play as long as we agree to join in with their 'make-believe' play world. This happens in the home and it happens in the foundation years. Children make natural use of imitation and role taking as means of understanding the world. We also make use of role whenever we adopt 'voices' for characters when we read to children, or alter the tone of our voice to create atmosphere and add meaning for the listeners. We sometimes 'pretend' to be cross or surprised when we talk to our class or individual children, and when we do this we often manage to signal that we are not being entirely serious – that we are 'playacting'.

Using role with Nursery children

Teachers can make simple and informal uses of role as part of their regular teaching across the agespan.

By joining in with dramatic play and using role to encourage talk, develop the children's ideas on and reflection about what is going on. If a group of children are playing with cars, the teacher might take on the role of someone whose car has broken down – can the other 'drivers' help her? Where is the garage? How will she get there? What shall she tell the garage owner? Who wants to be the mechanic who fixes the car? Who will help? Does someone want to wash my car as well? The teacher may also present emotions for the children to respond to:

'Oh dear, I don't know what to do. My little girl is waiting for me. She will be worried.'

This simple intervention by the teacher in children's dramatic play can be a very economical and effective way of delivering multiple learning objectives. By engaging children in a dialogue based on their play activity, the teacher can:

○ extend the children's imagination by suggesting developments and new 'twists' in the story they are making;
○ develop language, by modelling different registers of talk and directly engaging individual children with questions that require a response;
○ help children to understand the relationship between language and context;
○ encourage interaction and social learning in the group being worked with;
○ develop emotional literacy and sensitivity to the emotional needs of others;
○ model learning through dialogue and discovery and help the children to reflect on what they are doing in their dramatic play.

Using role with children in Key Stage 1

Teachers can use the story mat as a place for role play. We are used to stopping stories to ask children to predict what might happen next, to draw attention to some aspect of language, or to clarify the story for children. We can also stop and allow children to think about the questions they have about the story so far. Why did Goldilocks go into the Bears' house? Did she know it was the Bears' house? Would she have gone in there if she had known? The teacher then asks which character in the story they would like to answer these questions and says: 'All right then. You ask the questions and I'll answer as if I was Goldilocks' (or whichever character is decided on). The teacher doesn't need to act like Goldilocks, she merely uses the first person in responding to the children: 'I was lost and hungry and tired and wanted somewhere warm to rest.' But there is a magic in hearing your teacher respond as someone different, someone in the story. This magic can be used to develop conversations with the children: 'Have you ever been lost like me? What was it like for you?'

Using role with children in Key Stage 2

The teacher can develop this strategy for use in subjects such as history, by taking on the role of a character in order to give information. Without leaving the class-room, the teacher might take on the role of a 'street urchin' and describe her life and the conditions for children in Victorian times as an introduction to this period of history. This simple activity can be enhanced by the teacher using simple props and costume to give a stronger visual and 'authentic' feel to the role. Children could be asked to take on the role of 'time travellers' who must get as much information as they can from their meeting with the 'street urchin'. Their 'research' could then lead back to a more formal study of urban life in Victorian times. In Chapter 1, we used the example of Azmat to show how drama can make the remote cultural and historical significance of 'Tudors at sea' accessible and meaningful for pupils from different cultures.

Walking in someone else's shoes

By taking on roles that are different from themselves children, in these examples, are encouraged to speak, move, think and feel differently. What they say and do in-role is therefore determined by who they have become in the drama, where they are, who they are with, how they respond and what they are doing or thinking.

Acting and interacting (see Figure 5.1, opposite)

Social relationships are understood through acting and interacting with other roles. Children's choice of language is an expression of their character's need and intent, while symbolising their position on a social scale:

o Child takes on role of parent: she changes her register, becoming concerned or angry, the way she stands – holding out her arms, holding her head in her hands, etc.
o Child takes on role of wolf: she changes her voice, becoming gruff and deep, the way she moves – with a swagger, with confidence, with stooped shoulder, etc.
o Child takes on role of King: she changes her posture, sitting up straight, shoulders back, the language she uses, becoming authoritative and formal, etc.

For many children the experience of role and character becomes a 'lived experi-ence' and therefore one which children will be able to draw on at other times in their learning and living.

'Teacher-in-role'

In addition to these informal and classroom-based uses of 'Teacher-in-role', staff committed themselves to making a more sustained use of this strategy in drama sessions. Here, Helen describes her use of 'Teacher-in-role' with her Year 4 class as part of a drama project looking at the Aztecs:

Using 'Teacher-in-role' for 'Aztecs' project

Using 'Teacher-in-role' has allowed me to develop many learning issues with my children. They have become more explicit in their questioning skills, their language development has improved and they have become skilful in their observations.

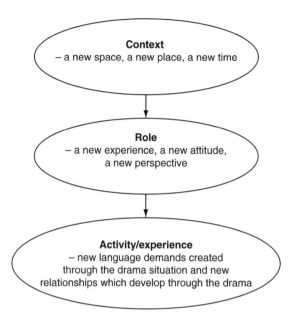

Figure 5.1   Role, character and experience

In my first drama session I took on the role of the Aztec Emperor Montezuma II. The children took the role of the Emperor's courtiers. The activity was delivered in a circle with myself simply wearing a shawl to show that my role had changed from teacher to Montezuma II.

The role of Montezuma II was used to develop the children's understanding of the Aztecs and their empire. I wanted the children to understand the importance of the Aztec leader and how he truly felt about the presence of the Spanish invaders. Children were invited to ask questions of the emperor and to offer advice as to how the Spanish might be defeated.

During the first session as Montezuma II, I felt very self-conscious and didn't really know what the response from the children would be. I had prepared and rehearsed in my head exactly what I was going to say but of course didn't know what the children's questions would be. I remember feeling very nervous and apprehensive. As it turned out the children were brilliant and really treated me as if I was royalty – even addressing me as 'Your Majesty'.

As I got to know my children and established a relationship with them my confidence to change the usual structure of a lesson and to explore new ideas progressed. I felt I was in a safe if unknown environment that would allow these changes to happen. The non-threatening nature of drama meant that I could attempt these roles and not worry too much if it wasn't completely successful.

Despite the predictable nerves and anxieties, the roles were intended to support and develop children's understanding of specific issues and this would allow me to address these in a way that would engage the children (even if they didn't participate they enjoyed watching me dressed up or adopting a different persona). I was also spurred on by the need to have a go and just simply try it out. Teaching is very similar to acting and so I looked at 'Teacher-in-role' as an extension of that. The children were attempting something new so why not work with them and give it my best shot.

Let us look more closely at what Helen's description tells us about working in-role. We will analyse the example using these headings:

1 **'Role-action' and 'Teacher-action':** How the teacher works at two levels – in the drama as a character who guides the story and as teacher who introduces specific teaching objectives into the activity.
2 **Setting the context:** How 'Teacher-in-role' can establish for the class the context of roles, situations and tasks that need doing.
3 **Responding in role:** How the teacher can use the role to respond to the pupils' contributions in order to both create challenge in terms of learning and also protect the class in-role so that they feel safe to contribute to the role play.
4 **Selecting a role:** How to decide on which role will be most effective in getting the class involved in the role play, setting the context and defining the work the class must do in-role.
5 **Introducing the role:** How to give clear signs to the class about when the teacher is in and out of role, so that pupils are not confused about when they are expected to respond in-role and when they are working normally as themselves with the teacher.

1 'Role-action' and 'Teacher-action'

Teachers are never 'in-role' in the same way as pupils. They have their other role of teacher to consider as well. In Helen's example, she uses the role of Montezuma to invite the pupils to take on the role of his subjects and to think, feel and act as they might have done. She wants them to imagine themselves as Aztecs facing the Spanish invaders. But Helen herself remains very much the teacher – guiding, controlling, encouraging participation, modelling language and behaviour.

Helen also lists some of the learning outcomes from drama for her pupils, the reason why the pupils have developed these skills in drama is because of the way she uses drama to teach. This means having a clear objective for both the use of 'Teacher-in-role', and also for the particular learning objective towards which the role play is intended to work. The teacher must also decide on a task in the drama for the children to do which will be relevant to her learning objectives.

For instance, Helen could use the role to create a context for looking at the structure of formal letters – she could have told the class that she has received a letter from Cortez and that the Emperor wishes to respond with a letter written in the same way as Cortez. A prepared letter from Cortez introduced as a 'prop' could be the model of formal letter writing, which the class then 'discover' and use to write a response in the same genre. In this way, Helen could manage the 'story' of the drama to lead children to an authentic learning task done 'in-role' which realises her teaching objective for the session.

Helen might have introduced a maths problem for the class through her handling of the drama. The 'Emperor' could have reported that spies had crept into the Spanish camp and counted 500 men. They also counted 750 bags of wheat stored in the camp. The Emperor's experts have calculated that 100 men will eat a bag of wheat in ten days. The Emperor asks his advisers to work out how long the Spanish food store will last them and what they think the Spanish will do when their supplies run out – will they get back on their ships and leave?

2 Setting the context and giving information

In order for teaching in-role to be effective, the teacher needs to do two things; set the dramatic context and set and keep to his or her own objectives for learning in the lesson.

Setting the dramatic context means being sure that every pupil understands what the fictional circumstances of the role play are. In theatre, these fictional circumstances are sometimes called the 'given circumstances'. The 'given' means that these are the boundaries within which children must agree to work together – they are unalterable. Making sure the children are clear about the boundaries of the 'given circumstances' of the role play is essential. They will not know what to do or say otherwise, and will cover their confusion with disruption. The circumstances are defined in response to 'W' questions. Using 'W' questions with children can also help them to see the structure of the role play and understand the relationship between context, language and action.

Before starting any role play, the teacher must ensure that everybody can give some answers to all of these questions:

o Who are we? (*Aztec warriors meeting with the Emperor*)
o Where is this taking place? (*In the Emperor's palace in Mexico*)
o When is it happening? (*A long time ago, before modern warfare*)
o What is happening? (*The Emperor is asking for advice from his warriors*)
o Why do we think it is happening? (*The Emperor knows that the Spanish are a threat to his empire and people*)
o What happened before this? (*The Spanish have demanded that the Emperor surrender*)
o What do we expect to happen next? (*There will be a battle which might be lost*)

The teacher can establish the 'given circumstances' in various ways. Helen could do it in her role as Montezuma: 'I, Emperor Montezuma II, king of all the Aztec people, have called you here to my palace courtyard. I ask you my most senior and trusted advisers for your help. The Spanish invaders draw near and we must decide what we should do before nightfall.'

Helen could also set the context out of role through a question and response session: 'Who was the most important Aztec?', 'Where do you imagine the Emperor would hold a meeting ?' 'Who would he call to the meeting?'

Once the context is set, children will know that what they say and do in the role play should be guided by the context – who they are in the drama and what is going on. The context can also be further established by using chairs, props, a few costume items and lighting if they are available. Pupils might do prior work on some of the 'given circumstances'; Helen's pupils had researched the Aztecs and made still images of their lives. They had established 'family groups' of farmers who supplied the Emperor's island palace through earlier role play work.

3 Responding in-role

In responding to the class in-role, Helen can shape the direction of the drama and use her in-role dialogues to:

o **Invite participation** – 'Has anyone seen these strange people who have come to our lands', or 'I have brought you here to seek your advice, who will speak first?'
o **Encourage participation** – 'The women of the village are very quiet – have you nothing to say to your Emperor?' or, 'And how about you, have you met the Spanish yet?'
o **Challenge** – 'Do you speak for everyone or just yourself' or 'How do you know these things, have you met the Spanish yourself?'
o **Get commitment** – 'We have hidden our treasures so that the Spanish will not find them, I need you to swear that you will not betray the secret hiding place to the Spanish, will you do this?' or 'Is there anyone here who is wise enough to know what we should do next?'
o **Persuade** – 'Unless we can come up with a plan we will have to surrender to the Spanish' or 'That's a good idea but you will have to speak to the others and get their support for your plan'.
o **Reflect** – 'Where have these people come from, what do they want from us?' or 'Will we be able to carry on living as we did before; will these invaders change our lives?'
o **Protect** – 'Listen to her, she may be right' or 'This is no laughing matter, take the words of your friend seriously'.
o **Respect** – 'Thank you for these words of advice, I will think about them carefully and meet with you again to give my answer' or 'I am disappointed that you no longer listen to your Emperor/each other'.
o **Close doors/open doors** – 'The Spanish are stronger than us and have better weapons; there is no point in suggesting that we attack them, what else could we do?' or 'Perhaps we could agree to meet with them and hear what they want from us?'

The key here is to try and get the right balance between challenge and protection for the pupils. There has to be some challenge for learning to take place. In Helen's example, the challenge for pupils is to use what they know about the Aztecs to propose what should be done; they also have to find the right language and gestures to communicate with the Emperor. But, as we have seen, the teacher can also protect those for whom this challenge is too great and also use her role to protect individual pupils from being laughed at for their suggestions.

Getting the balance right between challenge and protection is what creates the 'safe risk' of drama for both teacher and pupils, which Helen identifies when she speaks about being 'in a safe but unknown environment'. This will have been the experience for her pupils as well. Because Helen has created a 'non-threatening' context for learning in drama, her pupils feel protected enough to be 'brilliant' and to treat her as if she were truly 'royal'.

Getting the balance between challenge and protection is also important in terms of managing social learning in drama. You might find the prospect of becoming someone else a worry! However, like Helen, you will be surprised just how much more the class listen when someone 'new' has entered the classroom. The very fact that the teacher is taking the risk to become a character in the story is always positively welcomed, particularly when it is a role that is different from the teacher's usual position as the authority figure, the one who has all of the answers. Children enjoy interacting with someone new, someone different to the adults they regularly interact with at school. By working in-role you are giving pupils responsibility to behave and respond appropriately, and the opportunity to solve problems and to be of help and assistance.

4 Selecting a role

Helen chooses the high-status role of the Emperor Montezuma II, a role that echoes her own high-status role as teacher. She can use the role of the Emperor as she would use her role as a teacher to manage and discipline her 'subjects' if necessary – 'I will have order in my court, you will speak in turns or I will have to punish you all!'

In different circumstances Helen might have chosen a teacher role such as a humble Aztec messenger sent by the Emperor to the class in-role as warriors to warn them that strange invaders had been sighted and to prepare themselves for battle. She might have chosen the role of Cortez introducing himself to the class in-role as Aztecs. Thinking about the status of the teacher role is important because children will react in different ways to the Emperor, the messenger and the invader. They may be easier to control in the role of Emperor, more likely to want to talk and ask questions of the messenger, and may attack or shout at the invader!

It is important when selecting a role to work with, to consider the ways in which you want pupils to be challenged and protected so that they can be fully involved in the activity:

o What are the possible roles that I can choose from?
o Which role will best engage the class?
o Which role is most likely to get a meaningful response from my class?
o What will be my role objective, how will I use role to develop story and context?
o What will be my learning objective, how will I use role to set up a learning task?
o Do I want them to help the role or follow orders?
o Is the role going to offer the children advice and help them with their problems?
o Is the role going to make things much more complicated so that pupils have to think harder and work together to resolve problems and obstacles introduced by the role?
o What feelings do I want to draw on?
o Do I want to encourage an empathetic response or another emotional response such as frustration or disappointment?

Then you might want to consider if your role is:

o someone in a position of *authority*: a king or queen, a headteacher, a captain of a ship, or perhaps a police officer;
o someone *who is a threat*: a wolf, a bully, someone who is going to build on the local park;
o someone *in need of help*: Goldilocks, Badger protecting the young animals of his forest, a princess or prince held for ransom;
o someone who has come to *warn or advise*: a wise old woman/witch, a gatekeeper, someone who lives deep in the forest;
o someone who has *low status*: someone homeless, a lost child, a servant or messenger.

The most important consideration is which role is most likely to get a response in-role from the class? The teacher uses role as a way of moving the whole class into the role play. At the first opportunity the 'Teacher-in-role' should invite responses from the class and keep seeking involvement in the role play from every child. Once the class begin to get involved the teacher should respond to their contributions in-role. As Helen says, this can make teachers apprehensive because they don't know what questions they will be asked when in-role, or what suggestions the class will propose. But she also notes that children are very willing to accept and work with the 'Teacher-in-role' – it is a much more engaging and interesting learning style than sitting behind desks listening to teacher instructions!

The teacher's confidence when working in-role comes from her detailed knowledge of the role's background. In this example, Helen knows more about the Aztecs than the children so she can be confident in answering their questions. It is important to prepare a role in this way, making sure you have enough background information to expect the unexpected. Usually, teachers also have more advanced language skills than the pupils, which can enable them to talk their way out of difficult situations: 'I can't remember that, you will have to ask one of my advisers.'

5 Introducing 'Teacher-in-role'

Whether introducing 'Teacher-in-role' for the first time, or whether this technique is a regular part of your teaching and learning, it is always important to remind pupils what will signal the transition from teacher to the role. Helen uses a scarf to signal this transition. Alternatively you might begin by picking up a prop such as a telescope or a book. It doesn't really matter so long as you are comfortable with the transition from teacher to role and the pupils are clear. This is particularly true for young children who may find it difficult to work out what is 'make believe' and what is happening in reality. Sometimes, children will carry on in their role even after the teacher has come out of role.

Having a special chair, which the teacher returns to on once again becoming the teacher, can be useful. The children are instructed that whenever the teacher returns to the chair they must come and sit quietly, fold their arms and listen to the teacher – this strategy is also useful for controlling boisterous or over-enthusiastic role play. As in any situation where the teacher feels uncomfortable, the role play can be stopped and children can come out of role to reflect on their behaviour, or on what is arising from the role play.

'Mantle of the Expert'

In this section we look at another key way of learning through drama. 'Mantle of the Expert' refers to any drama situation in which pupils behave 'as if' they are experts who are asked to use their expertise to help others or to resolve problems. 'Mantle of the Expert' is an extension of working in-role and 'Teacher-in-role'; it uses many of the same ideas and strategies. But four special features are added to the other 'given circumstances' (see p. 97) which make up the dramatic context for the pupils' role playing.

These features are:

o There has to be an *enterprise* which the pupils set up and run as a 'business' – 'Mantle of the Expert' is about taking on the role of people who are good at doing their job in a professional way.
o There has to be a *client* who asks the 'experts' to solve a problem or deliver a service associated with their enterprise.
o There has to be a *problem* for the experts to research and come up with a solution for based on their expertise and experience.
o There has to be a *task tension* to give some edge and challenge to the expert's work: time may be limited; there may be awful consequences if the problem is not resolved; there may be hidden dangers in the work or special requirements that have to be included.

Examples of 'Mantle of the Expert'

Nursery

The teacher in the role of one of the three bears in 'Goldilocks' asks the pupils in-role as 'security experts' to make the bears home 'secure' after the break in by Goldilocks. In this example: the *enterprise* is running a security business; the *client is* the bear whose home has been broken into and the *problem* is how to make the house secure. The *tension* comes from dealing with the bears' fears and helping the 'Teacher-in-role' as one of the bears not to overreact and overdo the security – particularly when the 'bear' suggests electric fences and barbed wire! In order to give advice, the pupils ask their parents about security in their own homes and are given a tour of the school's own security devices and how they work. They are introduced to the concepts of locks, keys, alarms, fences and security lighting. In-role, the pupils present a plan for the three bears' house and how to make it safe while also making it a 'home' – not too much like a prison or fortress!

Key Stage 1

The class in-role as 'landscape gardeners' are asked by the 'Teacher-in-role' as the headteacher of a Special School to create a garden for her pupils, some of whom are visually impaired and some of whom use wheelchairs. The pupils are asked to use their 'expert' knowledge to design a suitable landscape for the garden and suggest appropriate planting so that all the pupils can enjoy and access the garden. The headteacher also wants pupils to be involved in looking after the garden.

In order for the landscape gardeners to present their plan to the headteacher, they must research: the needs of visually impaired and wheelchair-bound children; which flowers and plants might offer textures and smells for visually impaired people; how to design the garden so that it is interesting and accessible for wheelchair users; how sounds and textures might be used; how to design and build paths and beds so that wheelchair users can do some gardening themselves.

In addition to this work, pupils will also have to consider the maths of the project: how big the space is; how big beds and other features will be; how many plants will be needed, etc. They may also look in science at why plants have scents and which insects, like butterflies, might be attracted by certain plants. From a technology perspective they might also consider how to install a watering system on a timer so that the garden users don't have to struggle with hosepipes and watering cans, or they might invent their own self-watering system using collected rain water.

Key Stage 2

With the guidance of their teacher, the class establish their own travel agency, which offers specialist packages for tourists visiting their home city – in this case Leicester. The class decide on a name, mission statement, logo and advertising jingle for their agency. They write letters from satisfied customers to help establish the kinds of packages they offer. The 'Teacher-in-role' as the manager of the agency introduces two clients and their problems.

The first client is a local Community Elder who is organising a three-day visit to Leicester for a group of Bangladeshi teenagers who want the 'agency' to organise a suitable package. They want to know where to eat and worship, as well as which historical sites and places will give them the experience of Leicester as a 'multicultural' city. Because they have never visited England before, the group also need advice on local customs and how to mix with people of different cultures in the city.

The second client is a teacher in a local school in Leicester who wants the agency to organise a three-day package to London which will include accommodation and travel arrangements as well as suggestions for museum visits and visits to historical landmarks and various forms of entertainment in the city. When the class come up with a draft package, the 'Teacher-in-role' as 'manager' of the agency introduces a further tension. She forgot to mention that the children were all wheelchair users, so the package will need to be redesigned to meet their specific needs. This will involve the pupils in going back over every aspect of their plans to ensure that the transport and accommodation arrangements, as well as the places they have chosen, are accessible for wheelchair users.

Topic work with a difference

Teachers are used to designing topics for pupils which integrate content and skills from different areas of the curriculum. A topic like 'weather', for instance, can be used as an umbrella for work in a range of subjects. 'Mantle of the Expert' works in a similar way: the teacher decides on a real-life situation which requires pupils to use learning from a number of different subjects in order to respond to a real-life problem. But it is also different in ways that are particularly important in an urban and diverse school which is using drama as a wide-ranging school improvement strategy impacting on the quality of cognitive, affective and social teaching and learning.

The strategy is particularly effective for delivering core objectives for drama (p. 19). The real-world context makes learning meaningful and relevant for pupils. They are actively involved in learning through making and doing and their self-esteem and confidence is encouraged by being treated as 'experts'. The examples that we give all require pupils to look at situations from different perspectives which include the expert perspective of 'landscape gardeners', and the client perspective of a visually impaired child.

The 'Mantle of the Expert' strategy has these advantages over conventional topic work approaches to curriculum integration:

1 Pupils work in the same way as experts in the real world. They work on authentic problems, which require them to use prior knowledge to construct new knowledge.
2 The 'given circumstances' of the dramatic context offer a single context and situation for learning in different subjects – the situation itself acts as the 'glue' to hold together skills and content from a range of curriculum subjects. The 'real world' ways of working and problem-solving model the ways in which curriculum knowledge is used and useful in the world.
3 Pupils are given time to be absorbed in the situation and develop depth of understanding in working towards solutions to the problems they are given during the drama. They are able to apply and consolidate learning in real-life conditions.
4 The strategy encourages pupils to work in disciplines rather than in subjects: they work as scientists using the disciplines of science, or as geographers using their discipline to solve problems. Using the disciplines of science and maths strengthens pupils' contact with the world beyond school. Many of the 'Mantle of the Expert' projects used also involve pupils in learning from adults other than teachers; they work with 'experts' from their own communities and research by talking to community members.
5 There is a significant change in the teacher–pupil relationship with pupils working with their teacher as a 'senior colleague' involved in a shared enterprise. This relationship also encourages teachers to find an appropriate pedagogy based in skilful questioning and discovery methods of teaching.
6 'Mantle of the Expert' projects are based in the same principles of 'self-realisation' that inform the drama strategy at Shenton – together we can solve

these problems and get a real sense of authentic achievement that the completed work will have a value beyond test results.

7 Because the projects are based on the class establishing and running their own 'enterprise' there is a strong motive for social learning and a model for community entrepreneurship and 'business sense' which is important for urban communities in terms of raising aspirations.

Working with other drama conventions and techniques

So far we have focused on the basics of role play using the 'Teacher-in-role' both to guide and manage the role play and to plan how to use the role play for learning purposes. In reality, a drama is likely to include the use of other conventions such as still images, thought tracking and hot seating as well as the kinds of role play activity we have described in this chapter.

Using different conventions allows the teacher to plan for work in different groupings from whole class to pairs and individual work. Different conventions also allow for different kinds of exploration in the drama. For instance, hot seating and thought-tracking characters at different points in a drama allows for an exploration of inner feelings and thoughts as well as allowing pupils to express their own thoughts about the characters and situations in the drama.

A teacher will make a choice of conventions based on a number of considerations, as shown in Table 5.1.

Table 5.1   Reasons for choosing different dramatic conventions

Managing the Story Drama	**Establish the 'given circumstances' of the dramatic context:** eg in the Year 1/2 Scheme on Noah's Ark (Chapter 4 pp. 85–90) the teacher uses 'Teacher-in-role' as Noah in order to introduce the circumstances of the drama that follows ie a warning that the world will be destroyed
	Develop the story line (new characters and events): eg in the Year 4 Scheme on the Tudors at sea (Chapter 1, pp. 3–4)
	Work at a symbolic level: eg as a conclusion to the Year 5/6 Scheme on Noah's Ark the teacher uses the gesture circle (ritual) in which each child must find a simple physical expression as a means of reflecting on the drama

(continued)

Table 5.1   Continued

	Provide performance opportunities: eg in the Year 5 drama based on *The Conquerors* (Chapter 6) the class make still images to show how the villagers would prepare for the General, and what the General does when he arrives. The teacher now uses small group performances based on the transition from one image to the other in order to create a strong audience response to the consequences of war
Focusing Teaching and Learning	***Diversify working groups:*** eg in this Year 2 drama based on *Not Now Bernard* (Chapter 3, p. 54) the teacher introduced her class to drama and deliberately moved through a variety of groupings from whole group, to pairs, to small group in order to keep individuals attentive and break down gender and cultural barriers
	Deepen understanding and encourage critical thinking: eg the Year 5 class use still images and small group role play to explore how the villagers change the hearts and minds of the General and his invading army, in their drama based on *The Conquerors* (Chapter 6, p. 133). Their teacher now introduces a *duologue* based on a conversation between a child and a soldier in order to focus their thoughts and feelings about war and the role of warriors. When the class have shared their work, the teacher selects one pair for *thought-tracking* by the other pupils so that they can summarise and focus the work done in different pairs
	Consolidate learning: eg as a conclusion to the Year 4 drama based on *The Tudors at Sea* (Resource 5, www.fultonpublishers.co.uk) the teacher has the pupils write in-role, in various voices, in order to consolidate their learning about life at sea for the Tudor sailors. This writing includes letters, journals and poetry
	Introduce focused learning tasks: eg in the Year 4 drama work on the Aztecs (Chapter 5, p. 94), the teacher introduces a *letter* from Cortez in order to set up a formal letter-writing task done by the pupils *writing in-role* as Aztecs

Provide assessment evidence for planning:
eg in order to assess whether pupils have understood the
different historical perspectives of Sir Francis Drake's
character which have been introduced through 'Teacher-in-
role', pupils make *still images* which must show three
different sides to his character: pirate, explorer and thief

Alter the 'challenge/protection' balance:
eg in the Year 2 drama *Not Now Bernard* (Chapter 3, p. 52)
the teacher makes different uses of *still image* to illustrate
the loneliness of the monster, then to illustrate the
loneliness of Bernard. This proves to be an emotionally
challenging exercise so the teacher ensures a positive
outcome by having the class add family members and
friends to their images so that Bernard is no longer alone.
The teacher also uses *thought-tracking* so that pupils can
express how Bernard's feelings change

**Differentiate learning styles and for cognitive/linguistic
differences:**
eg a Year 5 class establish the travel agency for the 'Mantle
of the Expert' example on p. 103 by working in carefully
selected groups with different tasks reflecting different
learning styles and cognitive abilities: creating a logo,
creating an advertising jingle for the radio, making posters
advertising travel packages, writing letters from happy
customers

Make more effective use of time and space:
Teachers found that these conventions work well in the
limited space of the classroom and as 'quick' drama
techniques for use in subject teaching: collective drawing,
writing in-role, role on the wall, 'Teacher-in-role', hot seating,
meetings, 'Mantle of the Expert', objects of character, still
images, sound tracking, interviews/interrogations

Managing
Behaviour

Energise a group:
eg for the work on *Noah's Ark*, the teacher introduces the
game of 'Huggy' in order both to energise the class and to
get them physically moving. As the game develops, the
teacher adds the simple rhyme 'The Animals went in Two by
Two' to introduce the 'given circumstances'

(continued)

Table 5.1   Continued

Focus attention:
eg in the Year 6 drama based on *King Lear* (p. 109), the teacher has the class make *still images* and *objects of character* based on the theme of 'fathers and daughters'

Change physical, cognitive or emotional pace:
eg in Example 9 from the drama Sleeping Beauty, pupils are asked to move around the drama space and on a given signal are asked to create *single or group images* which reflect both character and environment. Prompts by the teacher include complex concepts like bad fairy/secret tower which pupils have to turn into physical representations. The final whole class image of the 'forest of thorns' is used to heighten emotions and create atmosphere for the drama that follows

Work around anti-social behaviours:
eg in Example 10 of the Sleeping Beauty work (p. 70), the teacher uses *environments* to give children a chance to work quietly and independently and to 'distract' them from problems through making and doing

Teachers used the book *Structuring Drama Work* by Jonothan Neelands and Tony Goode (2000) to help them in identifying and using different drama conventions and techniques. We have based the 'progression in drama skills and conventions model' (Resource 6 on the publisher's website www.fultonpublishers.co.uk) on this book. The authors describe over 70 conventions in detail, and many of these are appropriate to use with foundation and primary years. The conventions are organised under four headings:

○ Context building action.
○ Narrative action.
○ Poetic action.
○ Reflective action.

The idea is that teachers can select appropriate conventions to develop the drama in different ways according to the need to establish a clear context for the drama ('given circumstances'); the need to move the story on; the need for pupils to work symbolically and the need for reflection on the meanings and experiences of the drama.

In Table 5.2 these different actions and needs are listed, with appropriate conventions suggested for each. The conventions have been organised into groups, which represent four modes of dramatic action. These modes relate to specific needs required for participation in drama. Knowing, through practice, the types and the conventions themselves, gives both teachers and pupils choices about how to develop their drama work.

Table 5.2   Conventions and models of dramatic action (based on the work of Neelands and Goode, 2000)

Mode	Rationale	Need	Examples
Context building	Which either 'set the scene' or add information to the situation of the drama as it unfolds	A shared understanding of place, time, characters and other contextual information is crucial to quality of involvement in the drama	*Guided Tour, Still-Image, Role-on-the-Wall, Objects of Character, Collective Drawing*
Narrative	Which tend to emphasise the 'plot' or 'what-happens-next' dimension of the drama	Arousing curiosity about the story line and a sense of what will happen next. Moving the story on and changing the pace of the drama	*A Day in the Life, Hot Seating, Meetings, Teacher-in-role, Reportage*
Poetic	Which emphasise or create the symbolic potential of the drama through highly selective use of language and gesture	Pupils need to look beyond the surface of 'plot' and to recognise and create a symbolic dimension to the work	*Action Narration, Gestus, Ritual, Masks, Montage*
Reflective	Which emphasise 'soliloquy' or 'inner thinking' in the drama or for reviewing the drama from within	Participants need to reflect on the meanings and themes which emerge during the drama	*Giving Witness, Thought-tracking, Voices in the Head, Group Sculpture*

Using conventions to support role play – an example

We close this chapter with an analysis of a Year 6 drama that was designed as an introduction to Shakespeare's *King Lear*. In this analysis we track the progression from first activity through to reflection on key characters and their relationship to the play's central theme. What we want to show is that the plan for this drama is progressive – each activity is carefully planned to lead towards and build on prior work – it is a 'scaffold' which moves the class from first contact with the material towards a deeper engagement with the play's themes, which requires a confident use of language and higher order thinking skills.

There must always be a scaffolding logic to planning in drama. Each activity is carefully designed to move the class towards a deeper engagement and understanding of the content of the drama. Planning is not simply a question of moving from one convention to another for the sake of it. There is no point planning to begin with a *still image* and then following this with *improvisation* unless there is some clear connection in terms of the scaffolding of learning: a progression based on clear pedagogic reasons for moving from one convention to the next.

King Lear by William Shakespeare

Rationale

This drama was created to introduce Year 6 pupils to the work of Shakespeare through the play *King Lear*. Pupils were provided with opportunities to work actively with his language, while dealing with some of the key issues in the play, ie the use and abuse of power, loyalty and greed.

Task 1: Sword and shield

The work begins with a simple, energetic and enjoyable game. This decision is based on the need to energise the group, lure them into the complexities of the play through a fun activity and to begin to get the class to make unselfconscious use of Shakespearean language.

Ask the class to find a space and sit on the floor. Explain that they are going to play a game called 'sword and shield', but in order to play the game effectively they must first be able to deliver the following line with determination and confidence.

In-role, deliver the line to the class:

'Come not between the dragon and his wrath'

Ask them what they think it might mean (ie 'Do not get in my way when I'm angry'). When the class feels comfortable with its meaning, ask everyone to stand up on their feet and imagine that are drawing a sword from their sheath. Offer a physical example and then encourage everyone to practice their movement again until they are comfortable with this. Perhaps select one or two of the pupils to model particularly interesting and creative examples.

Next ask the pupils to deliver the given line as they draw their sword. Gather the group into a circle and ask for a volunteer to step into the circle. Explain that the aim of the exercise is for them to draw their sword and then deliver the rehearsed line. Using their extended finger as the tip of the sword they try to tap their opponent in the middle of his or her back. Once this has been achieved by either player, the game begins again.

Before beginning offer the class a demonstration with a volunteer from the class. Then everyone should find a partner and space to begin their duel.

Once the exercise is finished, ask the class to reflect on the activity in their pairs. What skills did they draw on? Concentration? Feeling more confident with the lines? Having fun with the language? Making the language more physical?

Task 2: Lines across the circle

Return to a large circle and allocate each pupil with a number. Explain that it relates to a line of text from the play *King Lear*:

1 'Blow winds and crack your cheeks.'
2 'Rage! Blow! You hurricanoes spout!'
3 'Rumble thy belly full.'
4 'Spit, fire! Spout, rain!'
5 'Oh, ho, tis foul.'

Ask the class to see if they can make any connections with the lines. What might they be about? Talk through the difficult words and allow the pupils to question their meanings. This could be done with a 'talk partner' before feeding back responses into the whole group.

Encourage pupils to experiment with the line they have been given and speak it out loudly to themselves or the person next to them until they feel comfortable with it. Everyone talking at once creates a comfortable climate for experimenting with unfamiliar text.

Next ask all the 'One's to say their line out loud. Repeat the activity for each line before beginning to experiment with different ways in which the line could be spoken – angrily, fearfully, joyfully, tearfully, etc. Lines could then be delivered while moving one at a time across the circle. As one person walks to someone else across the circle, that person should make eye contact with someone else before walking towards them. Gestures could be added to the lines making their movements fit with the delivery of their line, ie holding their head in their hands as they speak the line tearfully.

Ask all those with the same number to make a group. In their groups they must decide on a gesture to accompany their line.

Back in the circle, the groups share their work and everyone else watching must then repeat both the line and the action together until all the lines are completed. Experiment by overlapping the lines and actions until each group is animated in the circle.

Task 3: Thou art a boil!

This activity is designed to build on the confident and expressive use of language established in the first two activities. It uses rehearsal techniques designed to encourage actors to explore performance possibilities, but it is used here to help pupils make sense of the meanings of language by playing with different ways of performing it physically and vocally. The class is now working in pairs, which allows for more pupils to be actively engaged and which will generate a wider range of 'possible' ways of performing the lines. The focus on insults keeps the fun element going and again serves as a lure for motivating the pupils.

Around the drama space are a series of insults taken from the play *King Lear*. Ask the pupils with a partner to read each in turn. Ask them to consider which ones they like and why? What is it about the insult that interests them/makes them laugh, etc? Which words don't they understand? What might the words mean?

1 'Thou art a boil.'
2 'Brazen faced varlet.'
3 'You barbermonger.'
4 'Blasts and fogs upon thee.'
5 'A plague upon you.'
6 'You beastly knave.'

Then ask them to come back together in the circle with their partners and share their findings. Each pair must select a different insult each and try to remember it (although the papers with them written on will be left around the room). They are going to experiment in delivering the insult, considering the tone of their voice, gesture and facial expressions.

Next they are to deliver the lines to and fro to their partner. Allow one or two minutes to experiment delivering their lines under the following spatial conditions:

○ keeping as far away from their partner while they deliver the line and move around the room;
○ keeping arm's length at all times from their partner while they move around the room;
○ keeping back to back with their partner while on the spot.

Once each exercise is completed, ask how the space between them affected the way in which they delivered their lines. For example, did they raise their voices more when they were apart? Did their facial expressions become more intense when they were close up? Did they feel that words meant as much when they had their back turned to their partner?

Task 4: Fathers and daughters

There is a shift of gear now from simple confidence-boosting work on using Shakespearean language and making expressive use of voice and gesture to communicate the meanings of selected lines. Now the plan moves towards the heart of the drama session, which is the meeting with Cordelia. This activity is designed to focus the class on the themes of the play. The plan identifies the theme of love and loyalties between fathers and their daughters as one which is accessible for pupils and relevant to their own real-life experience of being children. Still images are used as an accessible means for children to translate their ideas and thinking into a visible and discussible text. The teacher will make skilful use of questioning when groups present their images to deepen and clarify their understanding of the theme.

Ask the pupils to consider:

1 how a father sees his daughter (eg obedient/loyal/precious);
2 what a father expects from his daughter? (eg respect/love);

1 how a daughter sees her father (eg strong/a leader/wise);
2 what a daughter expects from her father (eg understanding/trust).

Write down the pupils' responses. Encourage them to draw upon more 'universal' ideas of 'father and daughter' relationships. Turn their thoughts to things that they have read about in stories, seen on TV or heard from their friends and family.

Ask the class to consider what memories a daughter might have of bonding with her father (ie scenes of affection). For example, a holiday (collecting shells together), being taught to play a game, a favourite photograph that they had taken together, etc. Once an idea has been thought of, ask for some volunteers to re-create each moment. Then ask the pupils to draw the object which is most significant to that scene (eg shells, a photograph) and place it in the circle.

Task 5: Meeting Cordelia

This activity is at the heart of the drama. The first three activities have tuned pupils into Shakespeare's language and begun to focus their attention on performance. The previous activity has brought the theme for the drama alive and signalled to pupils what to look for and listen out for in this activity. The teacher takes on the role of Cordelia in order to introduce the plot and characters of the play. This is designed to be a very theatrical moment for the class. The pupils are given responsibility to design Cordelia's bedroom in order to consolidate learning from the previous activity and also to build the class's investment in watching and listening closely to 'Cordelia'. Whenever possible the 'Teacher-in-role' uses whatever objects or other details the class have put into their design for the bedroom as a way of valuing and using their contributions. The teacher's monologue mixes lines from the play with narration; because of earlier activities the pupils will be able to detect the role's use of Shakespearean language.

Ask the class to sit themselves down in a semi-circle. The teacher begins by telling the class his or her own interpretation of the beginning of the play up to the point in which the three daughters are asked to declare publicly their love for their father.

For example:

> 'A long, long time ago in this country there was an elderly King called Lear. Due to old age he had decided that it was time to divide his kingdom among his three daughters, Goneril, the eldest, Regan, second eldest, and finally Cordelia, who was the youngest and perhaps most favoured by the King. Once this decision had been reached he called all three of his daughters together in front of a whole host of Princes, Knights, Dukes, Lords and other such people of importance and asked his daughters 'how much they loved him'. In return their words of love would be matched accordingly with part of the Kingdom.'

Now explain to the class that together they are going to prepare a scene in which Cordelia (Lear's youngest daughter) is seen after an argument with her father.

Ask the class to imagine what Cordelia's bedroom might be like. Encourage the class to take an active role in setting the scene using objects that are available in the studio (eg stage blocks, chairs, sari fabric). Invite pupils to place the objects that were used in the previous task according to how much Cordelia has valued them (eg the photograph might be placed under her pillow).

Once everyone is happy with the room, explain to the class that you are going to work in-role as Cordelia as she writes her diary that same evening in her room. Explain that the role will begin when Cordelia reaches out for her diary.

> Dear Diary . . . How could he say such dreadful things to me? My father whom I have obeyed, loved and honoured always. But to ask a child 'how much' they love their father is not right. I can still hear my sister Goneril now: 'I love you dearer than eyesight, beyond what can be valued rich or rare, as much as child e'er loved a father.' Followed by my sister who says the same. Then all eyes on me and I say nothing. I cannot heave my heart into my mouth. I love him according to my bond; I am his daughter and love him like a daughter, no more, no less. Yes he has begot me, bred me, loved me and I return those duties back. 'So young and so untender? he said. But I know so young and so true. Finally, his face red and trembling, he points towards the door: 'hence and avoid my sight'. (Looking to the audience) So if that's what he wants then that is what he shall get!

Once out of role, ask the class to share their responses as to what they have seen and heard from Cordelia. What was she asked to do? What does she think of her two sisters? What does her father think of her? Why did he ask her such a question? Then after some discussion ask which objects from her bedroom might Cordelia take with her and why if she does decide to run away.

Explain to the class you will briefly return to the role of Cordelia to see how she responds to each of the objects that the class have talked about. Where possible try to integrate their thoughts and responses in the action which follows.

Task 6: Hence and avoid my sight!

This activity is designed as a plenary, or closure, for the drama session. The pupils consolidate learning in earlier activities in a task that also allows them time and space to reflect on the characters and theme from the play to which they have been introduced.

Ask the class to form a circle. On the surrounding walls are a number of lines taken from the play which Lear uses to threaten or hurt Cordelia. Ask each member in the class to read through them with the person next to them before selecting a line which appeals most to them. Ask the class to imagine themselves as Lear and how they might deliver this line to Cordelia. What is their tone of voice like? What is their body language suggesting? What expression is on their face?

1 'Hence and avoid my sight!'
2 'Nothing will come of nothing.'
3 'Mend your speech.'
4 'A stranger to my heart.'
5 'So young and so untender.'
6 'Wretch!'
7 'Better thou had'st not been born.'

Ask for a volunteer to imagine Cordelia writing her diary and to place a chair for her in the middle of the room with the diary on it.

Next ask the rest of the class to position themselves around the room and around Cordelia. They are to work on the scene as if these lines are going around and around in Cordelia's head and she cannot escape from the hurtful things that her own father has said to her.

Model for the class some of the ways in which they might deliver the line as well as asking for individuals to provide examples before the scene begins. To begin with each line is spoken only when they are tapped on the shoulder.

Now encourage the class to build the tension of the scene with voices slowly beginning to overlap. Experiment with the different ways in which the line might be said.

End the activity by exploring how the class feel towards Cordelia. Why has Lear behaved in this way? How do they feel about Lear? Is this how fathers should behave? What could a father have done differently?

6

Making a common unity: inclusion through differentiation

This chapter:

o considers what differentiation in drama means, and what its purposes are;
o stresses the need for differentiation in drama as a strategy for social and cultural inclusion;
o suggests strategies for including pupils with English as an additional language (EAL), with special educational needs (SEN), and those identified as gifted and talented (G&T);
o gives an example of how differentiation for these groups might be applied in a scheme of work based on a picture story book.

Drama as an inclusive learning activity

Strategies for differentiating learning in all areas of the curriculum are determined by the range of abilities and needs of the pupils within a given class. Drama is no different and demands as much attention as other subjects. Urban classrooms, in particular, stretch the teacher's aptitude in ensuring that the range of needs from the most able to the least able are catered for, while also ensuring that pupils who have been identified as SEN, EAL or G&T are supported, encouraged and challenged appropriately.

In Chapter 3, we focused on addressing the wide range of learning behaviours found in any class, and looked at the importance of contracting and creating a positive learning climate. In this chapter we want to focus on differentiation for learning. Of course behaviour and learning are interconnected – learning to behave and behaving to learn. It is also the case that behaviour, in one way or another, is at the heart of drama work. Drama is the art form that focuses on showing why people behave as they do, how their behaviours are culturally, socially and historically shaped. In order for these dramatic explorations of human behaviour to happen, our own behaviours as learners in the classroom often need to be explored as well.

In this chapter too, we emphasise drama as a social art form, and a social way of learning. Drama may not be the most appropriate means of targeting individuals and raising individual and specific levels of achievement, but what it is good at is teaching children how to work and live together socially. It is concerned with how individual learners work and live together as an effective social group. The curriculum tends to emphasise individual achievements; in drama, although we are concerned with the contributions that individuals make to the social health and effectiveness of social learning, we are more concerned with the 'class' as a unit of social learning.

In urban schools like Shenton, a class is often made up of children from different faith and home communities. In the classroom, children may form other informal but close-knit communities based on gender and friendship groups for example. Drama work must of course recognise and be sensitive to the different needs and claims for recognition of the 'communities' represented in the school. But drama also seeks to break down the boundaries between communities in order to seek out a common unity in living and learning together; a unity based on discovering what we have in common as well as what makes us different. This search for a common unity in drama is represented by the behaviour contract discussed in Chapter 3 (p. 40).

In keeping with this theme, we want strategies for differentiation in drama to prioritise social and cultural inclusion as much as individual academic attainment. We are concerned to outline various strategies that will ensure pupils across the ability range are included and actively involved in the social and interactive learning opportunities that drama offers. In our view, differentiation is about giving every child an entitlement to our five core objectives for drama (see Table 2.6, p. 32).

In other words, differentiation needs to ensure that every child has the opportunity to learn in personally relevant contexts; to be actively involved in their own learning; to express themselves meaningfully; to find confidence and self-respect in their learning and to work equitably with pupils who are different for themselves.

Drama provides an appropriate context for inclusive learning, because it does not require specific levels of cognitive ability or physical dexterity, nor does it require prior knowledge of drama. It is easier to manage drama as an inclusive learning activity than a subject where differences of ability are more visible and pronounced. Because drama stresses the collective achievements of a class rather than differences in individual levels of ability and performance, it focuses on combined effort. This acknowledges that children will have different strengths, in different domains of ability.

Drama also provides a context for developing and including a wide range of learning styles. It is a multimodal art form, using sounds, feelings, shapes, objects, gestures, images as well as written and spoken language in order to communicate meaning. It does not depend on language alone (like poetry, for example), or on sounds alone (like music). It uses the full range of symbolic languages.

For this reason, a teacher can plan for different preferred learning styles to be activated in a drama lesson.

Visual learning

Action:

o When introducing a role from history, eg Sir Francis Drake (see *The Tudors at sea*, p. 4, and associated activities on the website, www.fultonpublishers.co.uk) use PowerPoint to project a series of images relating to this character (for example, his birthplace, ships, portraits of him and his contemporaries) to help reinforce understanding of the role in relation to time, setting and context. The visual clues could be enhanced through costume or props, such as a ruff, a map, a telescope, etc.

Aural learning

Action:

o As the class rehearse their work, play appropriate music to help inform the mood and tension of the piece (see Task 5, *The Conquerors*, p. 136). This could also be played over the work as it is presented. The class could be asked to consider if the work is more powerful through music and image than in words and action.

Kinaesthetic learning

Action:

o Pupils are set the challenge of creating character through sculpting the body of their partner to create the desired effect (see Task 3 *Not Now Bernard* p. 54). This task creates an opportunity for pupils to develop skills in the physical control of the body through gesture and movement only.

We gave more detailed attention to the strategy of 'Teacher-in-role' in Chapter 5 (pp. 94–101) but we want to signal here that this strategy is key to managing differentiated learning in drama. Helen, a Year 4 class teacher, describes her use of role as a means for including and involving the whole class:

> My Year 4 class were exploring the issues of bullying through drama and we had spent some time discussing the body images of bullies. To make a comparison I invited a child to make an image of a bully in the centre of the circle. I then entered the circle and portrayed the image of a victim, cowering below the bully and covering part of my face with my hand. I then asked the children to describe my image and facial expressions. The responses were inspiring: *'You are lower than the bully'*; *'You look like you are crying'*; *'You're on the floor'*; *'You look like you need help'*. Wonderful!

By physically taking on the role of the victim, Helen creates a powerful visual image which is used to draw out responses in language from the class. 'Teacher-in-role' is an important inclusion strategy because while in role the teacher can target individuals and differentiate her responses in role so as to make sure that every child feels involved in the drama. In this case, Helen creates a strong and emotive physical image which the whole class will recognise and respond to.

When teachers present themselves as characters in the drama, working alongside the children in role, they can shape and control the drama to ensure that all pupils are able to become involved. In a fictional meeting, for instance, in which a teacher takes on the role of 'Mayor', or chairperson, he or she can challenge the confident, or pick out shy and reluctant pupils and ask them for a direct response; the teacher can monitor levels of understanding and add more information if required, or use the role to clarify the situation; or can appeal to the class at a 'feeling level' as Helen does.

While 'in-role', the teacher can also make use of props, costumes, light and sound to help establish the character. The 'role' is used to control the role play, so the teacher can stop when necessary and suggest other ways of working. If, for instance, it is clear that some pupils are confused in the whole class meeting, or not sure how to respond or get involved, the teacher can shift into pairs or group work and use the conventions of *still image* or *hot seating* to give every pupil the chance to be more involved in the drama.

Strategies for supporting the needs of EAL pupils

Meera, the drama co-ordinator, helps to put this discussion about drama and inclusive teaching and learning into context in her reflections on the experiences of EAL pupils in drama in the following case study.

Drama and integration

I feel that drama has played a key part in helping new children integrate into our school. It is a daunting experience starting a new school for any child, but the added pressure of not understanding the language and becoming accustomed to a new lifestyle in a new country is almost unimaginable.

For example Avanti started Year 3 in the middle of the academic year. She had very little English vocabulary or understanding of the language. Starting in the middle of the year made it particularly difficult for her to 'fit in' as children had already established their friendship groups. When she started she was shy and nervous, unconfident and very quiet. She only spoke on a one to one with me in her mother tongue. I was able to use drama to deepen Avanti's understanding (and that of the class as a whole) of issues like friendship, bullying, prejudice and co-operation. I noticed a dramatic improvement in her confidence and self-esteem. More importantly, she seemed happy participating in small groups.

It was also great to watch other children supporting her with her oral work. Together the class had learnt the importance of working together as a team, towards a collective aim, which could only be achieved by supporting each other. I felt she was accepted with ease by the class and this had a tremendous impact on her self-esteem.

Avanti soon became confident speaking English to the whole class. She had picked up a tremendous amount of vocabulary in a short amount of time. She used words like 'brave', 'unhappy', 'lonely', 'scared' and 'frightened'. I believe this was because she had the opportunity to understand through experience, followed by a chance to express those feelings through 'real-life' situations in drama. Drama provided the perfect medium for this to happen.

The motivation behind learning another language is based on the basic human need to communicate and be heard. In drama the context will often create a real purpose for needing to communicate. Because drama is so 'situational' it provides a means of giving all pupils, like Avanti, experience and knowledge of the relationship between language and context.

This is particularly important for pupils with little or no English. Language use in drama is always contextual, so EAL pupils can pick up additional clues from the situation, from gesture and expression, from tone, atmosphere and all the additional support offered by the 'conversational' and 'real-life' practice of language in drama. Because drama is group-task orientated, EAL pupils can be supported to make whatever contribution they can and then to enjoy the satisfaction and confidence of being part of a group presentation. This approach to learning English also focuses on the cultural differences that determine which registers and dialects the English consider appropriate to particular situations; the use of Standard English for instance.

The following strategies can be effective for supporting the needs of EAL pupils in drama.

Organising 'work/talk' partners on a language basis

Wherever possible, pair together those pupils who are less fluent in English with pupils who are confident in their use of English and also share the same home language. Remember it is easier for pupils to make mistakes in a pair than in front of the whole class.

Create access into small group situations

Allowing pupils to work in 'friendship' groups makes it far more overwhelming and or intimidating for a new arrival to become socially accepted. However by constantly changing the group dynamic (for example, mixing children with different abilities and of either gender) it will soon become accepted that you don't have to be friends to work together. This can take time, particularly in classrooms where children have been used to working on the same table or in the same ability group in the classroom; however they can and will adjust. Peer-reinforced language development is one of the strongest motivators for language learning. Not only is the pupil with EAL needs benefiting, but so too are those who are supporting, guiding and leading the learning of others.

Create opportunities to 'rehearse' responses and contributions

In the beginning, try to avoid activities that involve 'spontaneous improvisation'. Give pupils who are less confident in using English a chance to 'rehearse' what they want to say or do to give them confidence in their contribution. Responding spontaneously in an additional language is very difficult. When on holiday, most of us will use a phrase book to rehearse conversations in advance. In the same way, pupils can use word banks and bilingual interactions with peers to 'script' their responses. They can also use their bodies to show what they want to communicate and to support spoken expression.

EAL pupils need encouragement to find the confidence to speak out in drama. Making an attempt to communicate is more important than accuracy of expression and pupils' use of language should *never* be corrected in the public arena of drama. Being told you are wrong in front of your peers will probably silence you for a while! The teacher should also protect the EAL child from other pupils' negative comments on their use of spoken English – it is important to celebrate them 'having a go'. The teacher can model appropriate uses of language or in preparation for some event in the drama (eg 'Let's think about how we should speak to the Queen when she arrives').

'Scaffold' each task appropriately

Where possible ensure that each task is carefully structured to allow pupils to progress through it in manageable stages:

o interrupt the work regularly to recap on learning objectives and expectations for the task;
o make sure instructions are kept simple;

○ write up the subject specific vocabulary used within the task on the board to support pupils' understanding and future use of the terms;
○ allow pupils to progress at their own speed;
○ ensure that the task can be 'extended' to challenge more able pupils.

Make roles within a group specific where appropriate

Not only is this a good way of 'differentiating' the learning for all pupils, it also helps pupils to avoid defending or attacking an individual's ability ('Miss . . . she can't speak English!') Below are a number of roles that you might want to introduce to the class and allocate accordingly:

○ the observer;
○ the audience;
○ the director or the directed;
○ the sculptor or the sculpted.

Again if these are roles that pupils are made familiar with, they will be accepted as part of the teaching and learning process in drama as opposed to being recognised as a 'troubleshooting' device when pupils have already become marginalised or potentially disruptive.

If given the opportunity, pupils can also make effective 'teachers' and 'helpers' for their peers.

Plan tasks that draw on your pupils' linguistic diversity

Introduce short extracts of 'text' which have also been translated into the pupil's home language. This creates opportunities for pupils to work alongside each other to help respond to or explore the given task. Although this will involve extra time to plan, bilingual texts should be used as a positive addition to all pupils' learning.

Pupils should be encouraged to draw from their own cultural backgrounds to create characters which might relate to, or parallel, the characters or circumstances of others who are introduced in the lessons. Giving pupils the opportunity to develop characters from something familiar provides individuals with a voice of their own and a chance to take ownership of their learning.

○ It is important to actively encourage the use of 'home' or 'community' language in the drama work. This is a positive learning experience for all pupils which provides them with the opportunity to recognise and show respect for each other's home language.
○ Ignoring home language can make a difference to a pupil's willingness to participate and therefore impact on their 'self-esteem'.

Select material that reflects 'difference'

When selecting material to work with, try to select from texts, images or other resources which are both relevant and meaningful for your pupils. Use stories and images both from the cultures represented in the school and others, as a way of valuing 'heritage' and recognising identities that are different. Avoid distancing EAL pupils through content as well as through language. Remember that, in most instances, any activities or materials that are good for EAL pupils are good for all pupils.

Where appropriate, use visual images to support the work

Visual clues enable EAL pupils to make connections between words and their meanings. The following strategies are useful:

o present new, subject-specific vocabulary in both written and spoken form;
o try to create simple icons which might accompany regularly used terms or commands such as dramatic conventions or rules for managing effective behaviour;
o support tasks with diagrams or visual images using the whiteboard, other computer technology, overhead transparencies or handouts;
o select objects that are universally symbolic, or props that could be used to help reinforce character or meaning.

Where appropriate, add meaning through alternative signs and symbols

Appealing to the senses is an effective way of making or communicating meaning. You might want to draw on a range of alternative dramatic stimuli to help pupils communicate their own feelings or, alternatively, to develop greater understanding of situation or emotion.

o Lighting effects can alter the mood within a scene or help to create an environment.
o Appropriate staging can affect how we feel in a space (eg surrounding an area with chairs and/or stage blocks can make a character or the audience feel closed in and or threatened). Blocks can be used to indicate status, or barriers between people.
o Sound effects (recorded/instrumental/vocal) can help draw the pupils into 'feeling' about character, context and situation. A single repeated beat on a drum might heighten suspense, a chorus of wailing sobs and cries might indicate loss or separation. Either way meaning is made, appreciated and felt without words needing to lead the drama.

Create opportunities for physical expression

When planning a lesson, look for a range of opportunities for pupils to communicate through physical expression rather than always relying upon the spoken word. Tasks can be 'differentiated' accordingly to allow EAL pupils to concentrate first on developing confidence through gesture, posture and movement. Insisting on oral responses from new arrivals may affect their confidence later on down the line.

Support language development by creating word banks

Creating appropriate word banks for any drama work is an effective way of matching activities with the appropriate vocabulary. Word banks can be transferred into 'word walls', providing pupils with a point of reference prior to, during and after the drama.

'Model' the task for the pupils

Where possible avoid explaining too much through 'talk'. Rather, 'model' the task either through teacher/pupil examples or through small group work. You might want to do the 'modelling' yourself, but you can also draw upon support from those pupils who are more confident to demonstrate their understanding of the task. Activities such as these should be maintained throughout the lesson. Interrupt the work at various points to share good practice from different groups and/or individuals that you have observed. Not only does this help to raise levels of expectation, it also provides pupils with ideas for building into their own work.

Strategies for supporting the needs of SEN pupils

Teachers have become familiar with a wide range of learning and social behaviours associated with pupils who have special emotional, physical and learning needs. This range includes children who may be hyper-active and have short attention spans and who those who may exhibit aggressive or physically threatening behaviours if they get confused about what is happening or scared that they will fail. It will include pupils who struggle with language or conceptual thinking and pupils who work with restricted sight, hearing or movement.

More often than not those children who experience problems with their sight, their hearing or their mobility will have specialist support from either an outside agency or from an experienced LSA. These children's needs can be negotiated and prepared for in advance of any lesson so that they are able to participate actively and effectively in the work.

Gary is a behaviour mentor who works with class teachers in all years during drama sessions as well as in the classroom. Here he talks about his observations of Abdi in drama.

Challenging behaviour

Abdi was a new arrival from Sweden. As well as having little English he also displayed very challenging behaviour. He would exit the class, leave the school site, attack pupils and staff and damage school property.

I worked with Abdi during some of his drama sessions. In the beginning he would not stay in the drama studio for very long and he would run off. We were persistent in helping him back in to the sessions as we believed he would benefit from them.

In time he began to get more confident and would remain for longer in the studio. He became less disruptive and began to listen to teachers and other pupils. On several occasions he began to work with other pupils and participate. He also began to talk about drama. He would talk about the story and his feelings. On the social side, being able to interact with other pupils I believe helped Abdi to become more considerate and use more language to express his feelings.

Pupils like Abdi, with emotional or cognitive challenges, may respond to the active and practical nature of drama. They may also respond to the familiarity of learning through stories and role playing. In drama, pupils are given the opportunity to learn in context by physically making, responding to and shaping experiences. They are able to work with a range of emotions within fictional settings, and the teacher can skilfully select roles which will benefit particular pupils. The angry child can become a wise old woman or a crusading leader, the isolated can sit on the throne with servants to tend to their every need, the loud can become silenced by pirates searching for lost treasures, and the voiceless can be heard as they lead the search for the great white tiger. In drama, children can imagine themselves differently; they can be transformed and released from the labelling of special educational needs.

A child may have learning difficulties but this does not mean that the level of challenge should be reduced. All pupils can be pushed to work beyond their ability if lessons are planned to involve, engage, stimulate and progress the learner equally irrespective of difference.

The following practical strategies can be effective for supporting the needs of SEN pupils in drama.

Making the space safe

For some pupils, open spaces can be challenging, threatening, intimidating and perhaps most simply 'unpredictable'. Therefore managing the class's use of space is crucial in making the environment safe and welcoming for everyone. Priority should be given to making the working space 'environmentally friendly' with the use of displays of photographs, artwork or writing which has come from their drama experiences. There should be careful consideration of what is expected in the drama studio or space, in terms of which areas can be used and which are out of bounds, as well as warnings about moving slowly and keeping noise at a reasonable volume when working. These considerations will form part of the contracting process, so that all pupils feel reassured about their physical and emotional safety before moving into an open space for drama.

It is also important to use clear signals to indicate when the space is being used like a classroom for giving instructions and leading discussions for instance, and when it is being used for drama, for role play activity for example. The distinction between what is happening as drama and what is happening as more routine learning can be signalled by lights and sound or by moving from one area of the space to another. The teacher should also clearly signal when she is in role and when she is being teacher. She might put on an item of costume such as a hat or jacket to show she is in role, or sit in a particular chair when she wants the class to gather around her as pupils rather than as actors in the drama.

The circle as a symbol of common unity

It is important that pupils come to understand both the purpose and the power of the circle (p. 42). The regular use of the circle in drama can be very comforting for children with SEN. The circle helps them to see that there is no one person in front, no place to hide or sit apart from, and that everyone is equal. Everyone can see each other and the teacher is included in the learning experience rather than teaching from the front. The circle itself is symbolic to the subject and to the work, but this is not its only function. It is also central to the management and control of the class.

o Begin and end the drama work in a circle.
o Return to the circle between activities to re-group, re-focus and reflect.
o Present and perform work within the circle.
o Undertake activities in pairs and/or small groups while maintaining the shape of the circle, rather than spreading out and losing the physical contact between groups or pairs (particularly if you are working in a large hall or open space).

Work on creating a non-judgemental environment

This approach is particularly important when working with SEN pupils who spend much of their school life – and perhaps their home life too – being 'judged' by everything they say and everything they do. When we feel that we are being 'judged' or 'tested' by others, in particular by the teacher or by our peers, there is pressure to succeed. This can make learning appear to be something we either 'pass' or 'fail'. In drama it is essential to emphasise the collaborative and inclusive nature of learning. As a teacher, therefore, you might want to:

o remind pupils that you are a learner too;
o avoid asking closed questions that require a right or wrong answer and find ways of integrating responses to open-ended questions into the drama even if they first appear to be based on a misunderstanding of what has been asked for;
o write down the contributions that pupils make or alternatively illustrate them through image rather than always reacting verbally;
o allow for silences when a question has been asked, make 'thinking time' real and purposeful for pupils;
o emphasise the collective nature of the work – for example, what we are going to do together rather than what you want individuals to do. Additional 'scaffolding' for the less able should be discrete and not draw attention to their 'deficiencies'.

Consider the importance of transitions

What happens between activities or tasks is as important as what happens during them. It is the transitional periods that allow pupils to lose concentration, look for and find distractions.

o Return to the circle to reflect, share and/or evaluate the work.
o If appropriate, recap on learning objectives to refocus the purpose and value of the work. Use music to create seamless moves from one activity into the next.
o Ensure that one activity informs the next, thereby sustaining interest and making progress visible. The logic of the sequence needs to be made clear for less able pupils in particular; often this logic will best be understood in the context of a narrative or ongoing story about what we are doing – 'So what would happen next then?'

Discovering the use of ritual

Ritual is used regularly and successfully in drama with children who have moderate to severe learning difficulties. Due to its stylised nature and the fact that its success is determined by traditional rules and codes, ritual is a great way to encourage involvement and strengthen engagement in the work. Because rituals have a quiet and serious feel to them, they also work as an effective behaviour management tool for hyper-active pupils. Pupils are made to feel safe due to the group culture, which is often associated and created through ritual as well as the repetitious and therefore accessible nature of the work. (See Task 10, *The Conquerors*, on p. 139 for an example of ritual.)

Using gesture, mime, visual symbols and images

Because drama is a multimodal form of communication, meanings can be conveyed physically and visually as well as through verbal and written forms of expression. Pupils can show how a character feels, they can draw characters and settings, they can work with objects as symbols for ideas (a key to represent freedom for example). Whenever pupils struggle to find the appropriate words or concepts, they can be asked to *show* (rather than say) what they mean. Symbols can also be used to represent the rules of the contract or to represent familiar conventions such as *still images* or *thought-tracking*. The teacher can compile an ongoing story board of simple drawings to remind the class of what they have done, or make digital images which can be used to remind children of what they did in the previous lesson.

Providing alternative roles

Like any other subject, drama has its own trigger points for exacerbating particular behaviours, including aggression, attention-seeking or withdrawal, which might interrupt the flow of work or progress of others. These behaviours are often revealed during small group work, in performance, and while working with unfamiliar and exciting resources such as fabric or musical instruments. Be prepared to allocate 'alternative' roles; for example, any child could be given the role of:

o **observer** – who watches the work with creative and constructive criticism;
o **photographer** – who captures the work in progress;
o **designer** – who interprets the drama through set, lighting or costume design;
o **co-director** – who helps the teacher to organise groups or model a task;
o **helper** – who holds props, instruments or books for the teacher, or who will take messages to groups who are working.

Strategies for supporting the needs of G&T pupils

Smita, the literacy co-ordinator, describes the enrichment and vital life-skills learning that drama has offered to Suhayl, a G&T pupil who has exceptional ability in maths.

A 'whizz' at maths

Over the year, Suhayl has made tremendous progress because of drama. Suhayl is a 'whizz' at maths, especially when it comes to mental arithmetic and problem-solving. He manipulates numbers quickly in his head and comes up with the answer before anyone else.

Generally he got on with most pupils in the class and was popular among the other boys, but when it came to working in pairs or small groups he was unable to co-operate, share ideas or make valuable contributions. This has made other children unwilling to work with him, so he tended to misbehave in these situations and would often end up working on his own.

At first Suhayl found it really difficult to cope with the new way of working in drama, which involved lots of group discussion, sharing of ideas and co-operating with others. I tackled this by making him work alongside the classroom assistant, who would help him to listen and value other people's ideas and opinions even if he didn't agree with them. She supported and helped him develop his own ideas and use them to make interesting and sensible contributions to the group work.

Suhayl's attitude to group work has altered. He realises that there isn't always a right way of doing something and that everyone has something different to offer. The different learning styles used in drama have helped Suhayl to work more effectively with his peers. His skills in listening, compromising and negotiating with others have improved over time.

This has had a knock-on effect in other subject areas too. Not only is Suhayl more willing to respect and work with others, the new skills he has developed through drama work have complemented his talent for numeracy. He is now able to explain how he has worked out solutions to problems, and be patient with those who don't understand at first. He is much better at playing maths games in pairs or small groups. He has also begun to think of new and interesting ways to find solutions to maths problems.

Drama can offer a valuable process of enrichment for a wide range of G&T learners. Pupils who, like Suhayl, are exceptionally able in academic contexts such as maths, English or science, now have opportunities to apply their expertise to the real-life contexts of the drama. Talent in the visual arts and dance and music can be incorporated into the drama work so that talented pupils lead dance work, design or draw settings, characters, maps, and use musical instruments to accompany the drama and heighten atmosphere.

Creativity is an essential part of 'giftedness' so G&T pupils need the opportunities provided by drama to apply their thinking skills and abilities to real world situations and problems. They also need to develop their skills in the use of the symbol systems of drama and the other arts both to extend their cognitive ability and as a means of shaping and expressing their ideas at a feeling level.

Pupils like Suhayl will need less scaffolding and less stimulus than some other learners. This can make them very useful in helping the rest of the class to imagine, or understand or build on the clues suggested by the drama. Motivation is another key part of 'giftedness'; drama can motivate higher-order thinking, and problem-solving based on the curiosity to discover what will happen and why things happen as they do in the fictional context of the drama. G&T pupils often show a precocious interest in adults and adult affairs, sometimes preferring adult company to that of their own age group. Drama allows all children to work as adults, facing adult problems with adult responsibilities. This feature may arouse considerable curiosity about the human condition in G&T pupils.

It is also important for G&T pupils to make connections between subjects and between the curriculum and the broader world; gifted pupils need to be encouraged to look at the 'bigger picture' – at how subjects like maths and science help us in the world now and in the future. In particular, during the primary years they need to start thinking of subjects in terms of 'disciplines': what is distinctive about 'doing' geography for instance, or what does it mean to think and act like a scientist or mathematician. Drama can help in this process both by creating fictional contexts in which pupils imagine themselves to be adult scientists who have responsibility for solving a problem in the world through science, or by getting pupils to apply what they have learnt in the classroom to real world problems (see the section on the 'Mantle of the Expert' in Chapter 5, pp. 101–105).

The uncertainty of drama, in which pupils are asked to respond to open-ended questions, and to negotiate the outcomes of the drama, can be challenging for academically gifted pupils like Suhayl who do best when there are only right or wrong answers, rather than shades of grey. These pupils can usefully be taken outside of their learning 'comfort zone' and challenged by the idea that there are sometimes no right or wrong answers.

Because drama is a social way of learning which makes the most of everyone's 'gifts' and 'talents', it is an ideal forum for G&T pupils to learn about their social and moral responsibilities. Pupils who are identified as 'gifted' need to learn that they have a responsibility for using their individual 'gifts' to benefit their community, to be self-sacrificing and particularly to help those who are less able than themselves.

The social processes of learning in drama, the emphasis on community and the frequent focus on how collective action may resolve tensions, problems and dilemmas in the fiction of the drama, provides G&T pupils with the opportunity to practise leadership and demonstrate expertise without ego. Because of the focus on human behaviour G&T pupils can be encouraged to think about the ethics and morality of actions and their consequences. It reminds them that, in the future, their communities will turn to them for advice, social and moral leadership and support because of their talents – and that they need to learn how to respond with grace.

The following practical strategies can be effective for supporting the needs of G&T pupils in drama.

Talented work beyond the classroom

There will be pupils in your school who are talented in drama as actors, writers, and directors. Many children attend local drama and/or dance groups out of school, and some have the opportunity to take graded tests as benchmarks of their talent if they can afford to do so. In our experience, it can be difficult to respond to the specialised needs of these talented pupils in curriculum drama time. Of course, there will be opportunities for developing the skills of acting and directing, but in curriculum forms of drama we tend not to isolate performance skills for technical training, neither do we draw attention to individual skill attainment in vocal and physical techniques for instance. Talented young performers need specialist training and pathways to advanced training like young athletes. The additional needs of talented young performers are met through:

○ extra-curricular drama clubs and performances;
○ regular theatre visits;
○ visits and workshops from artists, theatre companies and graduate students of drama;
○ provision of information about local arts groups and organisations.

'Busy Bees'

Giftedness is associated with high levels of motivation. Gifted pupils tend to seek learning beyond the classroom and after the bell – they thrive on learning and developing their expertise. Talented musicians, for instance, must be motivated enough to practise for hours each day. Pupils can be asked to do tasks on behalf of the group, to research, to write a script or other text for use in the drama, to make a prop of a picture, to create a 'diary' or 'letters' belonging to a character. Pupils may also be given responsibility for sound or lights, or for making a CD of images and sounds for the drama.

Modelling and mentor

In drama we expect to make the best use of each pupil's 'gifts' – to find opportunities for each to perform to their potential. We make use of the skills of G&T pupils, and remind them of their social responsibility: by asking them to scribe, or to work bilingually with a new pupil; to chair a discussion, be responsible for feeding back or summarising a group's work; to describe in words what they see and experience in drama; to take responsibility for projects, and rehearse moral and social leadership in real-world situations.

A differentiated lesson for Key Stage 2

The following lesson, based on David McKee's *The Conquerors*, is used to demonstrate how drama lessons can be differentiated to meet the needs of EAL, SEN and G&T pupils. The story is about a country that conquers all other surrounding countries under the leadership of their General and with the help of their Big Cannon, until there is only one small country left unconquered. In the story, this small country does not fight or resist the conquerors, instead they welcome them and slowly introduce the 'conquerors' to their own culture. In time, the 'conquerors' are themselves conquered by the kindness and customs of the small country.

The Conquerors: Sequence of drama tasks

Rationale

This drama was designed to help Year 5 pupils to develop their speaking and listening skills, but more importantly providing them with the opportunity to explore complex issues which are of particular relevance today in multi-faith schools.

Starter Task: 'Follow my leader'

Begin by playing the game of 'follow my leader'; once the pupils are used to the game, you steer it towards the movements and actions of soldiers, by marching, halting, saluting, shouldering arms, etc. Gradually the pupils form into ranks following the teacher. You shift from game into drama by 'halting' the troops, standing them to attention and speaking to them 'in-role' as the 'General'. The General reminds them that they are the best army in the world. He tells them that tomorrow there will be a great battle and when they win they will have conquered another country. He asks them what they will need to do to prepare, then sends them off to do the tasks they suggest before calling them back, debriefing and sending them to their tents for sleep. The activity ends when all the 'soldiers' have found themselves somewhere to sleep under the stars.

o **EAL:**   The game-like format of 'follow my leader' will be familiar to most pupils, and will be easy to pick up as the activity begins. Actions speak louder than words and help give physical and emotive clues regarding the content and context for the lesson.
o **SEN:**   The task of mimicking the teacher is non-threatening and enjoyable, ensuring that everyone can be involved without the attention being focused on any one individual. The instructions given by the General are made explicit and followed by the whole class. In-role, there is the opportunity for the teacher to ensure that everyone in the group is included through targeted dialogue to humour, manage and challenge particular individuals.
o **G&T:**   Although this is a fun activity it relates to the very real and serious business of war. G&T pupils should be encouraged to reflect aloud on what it means to be a soldier, what anxieties they might have, what their concerns might be before a battle. This will stretch the most able and add to other pupils' belief in, and understanding of, their roles.

Task 2: The General's parade

Look at the first picture of the General leading a parade of soldiers and the cannon past the smiling crowds of his own country and read the accompanying text:

> There was once a large country that was ruled by a General. The people believed that their way of life was the best. They had a strong army, and they had the cannon. From time to time the General would take his army and attack a nearby country. 'It's for their own good,' he said, 'So they can be like us.'

With a 'talk partner' (see p. 43) explore the following questions:

(see p. 43)

○ What can we tell about the General and his people from this picture?
○ What emotions are expressed and why might that be?

Look at second picture, which is of a violent and bloody battle between the well-armed 'conquerors' and the people in one of the countries they are invading and read the text.

> The other countries resisted – but, in the end, they were always conquered.

With a 'talk partner' explore the following questions:

○ What does this picture tell us about the General and his people?
○ What emotions are expressed, and why might that be?

Access to the text and understanding of its context is reinforced during this activity through the illustrations in the story book. This is particularly helpful for EAL pupils. The pictures offer an insight into the key themes and issues which can prompt and support some discussion in 'talk partners' before feeding back and/or listening to others' ideas.
(NB: The use of 'talk partners' creates an opportunity for all pupils, in particular EAL pupils, to engage in discussion stimulated by the pictures. This is a chance to try out ideas before taking additional risks in a whole group environment. Pupils with EAL could respond to the pictures using their home language to help increase confidence.)

Task 3: Meeting the Mayor

Read the section of text describing the General's arrival into the small country. Ask the class to imagine how the people of the small country might react. Call a meeting of the people with 'Teacher-in-role' as Mayor. The Mayor has heard the General is coming; he doesn't know what his people should do; there is no army, no preparations have been made at all and there is not much time to act.

Invite the rest of the class to take on the role of someone in the village. Before getting into role, discuss what types of people might attend the meeting and how they might react to what the Mayor has to say. Once 'in-role', the villagers must explore what their options are in light of this news.

This activity enables pupils of all abilities and needs to both participate and contribute in a variety of inclusive and alternative ways.

o **SEN:** In this instance contributions need not always be verbal. The individual can show their involvement through their use of body language and gesture – for example, hiding behind somebody to show their fear of being attacked by the soldiers or raising their fists in agreement with those who are preparing to fight.

o **G&T:** Role can be used in this instance to heighten a pupil's use of persuasive language. For the example, the Mayor might target the G&T pupil:

> 'If you are confident that this village can sustain an attack from the soldiers then I ask you to persuade these people who are now cowering in corners or who cover their heads with their hands in fear to join you in defeating the General's army. Go on prove yourself; turn to the people and convince them you can win.'

Task 4: The soldiers arrive

Divide the class into groups of four or five. Each group must decide on one of the 'options' raised at the meeting (to hide, to try to discuss matters with the General, etc). Then the group needs to make a *still image* of what events would look like to the General and his men when they first approach the village.

Provide each group with a piece of paper and a pen. Once their image is complete they need to create a 'statement' which accompanies the image. This statement should represent the voice of the villagers. For example 'We will not hide from you!', 'Leave us in peace!', 'We surrender!'

Each group presents their image and statement and discusses its potential with the audience.

o **G&T:** Identify the G&T pupil or most able in each group and ask them to act as spokesperson for the group. Their task is to take responsibility for leading the discussion about the potential of the group's 'option' and accompanying statement. The audience could also be invited to question the spokesperson further on the group's choice.

After each image is presented, select another group and give them the choice to change the image into how it might look after the General and his men have seen it and reacted to it. For example, if the image shows villagers hiding in the church, another group may decide that the General would turn his cannon on the building. This would turn the image of people hiding into an image of the destruction caused by the cannon. If a group decide to show an image of surrendering villagers waving a white flag, another group might decide that the General would tie them up as prisoners or worse. Of course, the 'Teacher-in-role' as the General – or a pupil in the role – can give warnings to those hiding to give them the chance to escape first, or intervene to spare the lives of the prisoners and avoid unnecessary carnage!

You might use an opportunity like this to target the G&T pupil to demonstrate how they might change a particular image and what impact they want to create for the audience in doing this. This develops both critical judgement and the relationship between consideration of actor and audience.

Task 5: 'We all fall down'

Once each group has presented their work they must return to their groups and consider the image they started with, and this image was altered after the General and his men had arrived at the scene.

Explain to the class that you are going to play an extract of music. Ask the group to listen carefully and respond to the music with suggestions about how it made them feel, what it reminded them of and how it might link to their scenes. Choose something fairly mournful and slow.

o **EAL:** The use of music in this instance creates an opportunity to reinforce the learners' understanding of the piece. Not only is meaning enhanced through tension and atmosphere, the opportunity is also given to emphasise meaning through movement and action rather than words.
o **SEN:** The alternative role of 'sound technician' or 'lighting technician' could be provided for an individual who is struggling to maintain concentration in the group work or has experienced difficulty engaging with the task. This new responsibility for controlling the sound or lights enables the pupil to re-engage with the work from a different perspective. Although they are not directly involved with one group they are supporting the development of others' work as well as developing new skills and subject knowledge.

As the music is played for a second time, each group must consider carefully how they are going to move from one image into the next. This activity must be done in slow motion and should be modelled by the teacher. Encourage each group to count down from 20 as they move from one image into the next. Make the suggestion that someone stands outside the group to see what the transformation looks like and how it might be developed: should greater attention be given to changes in facial expressions, for example?

o **G&T:**   Release the G&T, or most able pupils, from each group to work 'in-role' temporarily as 'directors' of the group. Not only does this create the opportunity to reflect on and extend their critical capabilities with regards to subject content, but also demands are made on leadership skills and developing an awareness and sensitivity to the individual needs of others in the group and how best to support/direct them in performance.

When they are ready each group silently performs their work, one after the other, without pauses and to the music.

Task 6: 'Talking pictures'

Read from the story book:

> The small country surprised the General. It had no army and offered no resistance. Instead, the people greeted the soldiers as if they were welcome guests. The General installed himself in the most comfortable house, while the soldiers lodged with families.

Together the class make a *collective image* of the illustration, which accompanies the text. This is a panorama of the village, with the villagers talking to and welcoming the soldiers. Pupils take up the same physical position as one of the villagers or soldiers in the picture. This could be done in pairs so the individual children have the support of a buddy in making their choices and entering into the whole class image of the village.

When every pupil has found a place in the collective image based on the picture, they are asked to improvise conversations between the villagers and the soldiers. The improvisations should be based on:

o clues in the picture;
o their own physical position.

Once groups have had the opportunity to rehearse their conversation, move around the class to listen to bits of each conversation. This can be done by clicking your fingers over a group to start them and then clicking them again to stop the conversation.

o **EAL:**   Here pupils use the image to direct their work. Not only does the image model the character for them, informing their choice of body language and gesture, it also increases their willingness and confidence to actively participate. In any case, the villagers and soldiers may speak different languages and this could be built into the context for the activity.

○ **SEN:** The teacher can support and guide pupils to identify a particular figure in the picture and then help them take the same position in the collective image. SEN pupils might be given the first choice of characters to choose, or the teacher might discretely pair with a more able pupil: 'Siham, why don't you be the soldier who is talking to that woman over there.' The teacher in or out of role as a villager/soldier can encourage conversations: 'Can you tell me where your leader is?' 'What have you heard about the General and what happens when he arrives in a new country?'

○ **G&T:** The teacher can target pupils for reflective ideas: 'Why do you think the villagers are so welcoming?' 'Will the soldiers be suspicious of the welcome they are receiving?' They can also be asked to reflect on all the conversations and provide a summary of the different thoughts and feelings they have picked out of these conversations. Again, this challenges the most able while also contributing to belief and understanding of the situation represented in the drama.

Having heard each group, select individuals to *thought-track* focusing on their private thoughts in response to the conversation in which they have been involved. For example, one villager may feel about a soldier: 'I do not trust this man. Maybe he isn't coming here in peace'.

The task of thought-tracking can be made more complex for G&T pupils. For example, the teacher could ask pupils to consider the length and detail of their response, and also the way in which thoughts are orally delivered, giving thought to pace, pitch, tone and accent.

Task 7: Living in peace

Read the following from the story:

> The soldiers talked with the people, played their games, listened to their stories, joined in their songs, and laughed at their jokes.

Divide the class into groups (of three, four or five) based on the groups they made for the *collective image* in Activity 6. Ask the groups to consider what the soldiers might have learnt from lodging with the families in the village. Each group creates a short scene (no longer than a minute) which shows how the soldiers learnt to live peacefully with the villagers and what they might have learnt about their culture. This might be something which was mentioned in the text – a new game, a story or an idea of their own, cooking a meal, meeting relatives.

○ **SEN:** Work here is already informed by the choices made in Activity 6. The more opportunity pupils are given to build on work previously created, the greater will be their understanding and involvement.

Task 8: What does a soldier do?

How hard was it for the soldiers of war to trust and settle down? In pairs, improvise a conversation between a soldier and a child who asks: 'What does a soldier do?'

First, consider what questions the child might want to ask the soldier. Then, in pairs, either explore answers to those questions or encourage the pupils to ask further questions of their own. Share some of the work with the rest of the class.

o **SEN:** The fact that this work is undertaken in pairs can provide some pupils with increased confidence to carry out the task. Pupils could prepare the questions together before working on them 'in-role', similarly the responses could be explored together before they are then explored 'in-role'.

o **EAL:** Pupils with little access to English could work with a partner who can speak both English and their home language. In this activity the questions might first be asked and answered in the home language and then translated into English.

o **G&T:** The teacher could choose a G&T child to model this exercise with. Or the work from the pairs could be summarised by finishing with a dialogue between the 'Teacher-in-role' as a child and the G&T pupil as the soldier. Reflection for the whole group can be deepened by this exercise, especially if the 'Teacher-as-child' asks some really difficult questions: 'Why do soldiers attack people?' 'How would you feel if soldiers invaded your country?'

Task 9: Objects of character

Divide the class into groups of five. Allocate each group a description of who they are going to be – soldiers, parents, teachers or children. Each group finds an 'objective' for meeting and must await the arrival of the General before they can begin their meeting. Explain to the class that you are going to appear in each group 'in-role' as the General and together you will improvise the scene. Each group takes it in turns to have a meeting with the General, who begins to respond and listen to their concerns.

Task 10: Ritual gift giving

Look at illustration of 'changing the guards' which shows the General replacing the soldiers who have become the villagers' friends and companions. In pairs, imagine what 'gifts' or 'symbols' might be given as leaving presents between villager and soldier. These chosen objects are then drawn on paper. Then invite the class to swap partners and make two lines facing each other on opposite sides of the room. These gifts (pictures) are then exchanged in a 'ritual'.

○ **EAL:**   The use of objects and symbols in this activity over dialogue helps to reinforce an understanding of the relationship between the villager and the soldier, ie toy soldier carved from the wood of a tree in the village/a painting of the village.

○ **SEN:**   Some pupils will find access to the task and achievement through the responsibility of selecting and drawing the object. They will be able to draw on and demonstrate other skills and enjoy the independence this creates.

○ **SEN:**   The ritual of 'gift giving' will help to establish a safe and secure environment for a public sharing to take place. The stylised enactment is bound by tradition and rules which can enable some pupils to participate with a high degree of confidence due to the repetitious nature of the event.

As the ritual comes to an end, discuss what has been gained and lost in this exchange. How do soldiers feel about returning to killing? How do the villagers feel knowing their 'new' friends are also trained to kill?

○ **G&T:**   Questions such as this one will provide the G&T pupil with an opportunity to engage in higher-order thinking and debate with their peers and the teacher. The question can also be used to stimulate additional research and consideration beyond the lesson.

Differentiation checklist

Table 6.1 gives a checklist for assessing whether differentiation has been effective in creating an inclusive learning experience for pupils in drama.

Table 6.1   Differentiation checklist

	Y/N	Comment
Was the drama space safe and welcoming?		
Did I use the circle to show unity within the group? At what stages?		
Did my planning cater for a range of preferred learning styles?		
Were there 'alternative' roles for pupils to take on besides the role of 'actor'? What were they? Why and when were they used?		

Did I plan tasks which drew on my pupils' linguistic diversity?

Where possible did I use visual images/aids to support pupils' understanding of a given task?

Were word banks made available during the drama work for pupils to draw on during the lesson or build on in response to the drama work?

Were there opportunities for pupils to demonstrate and model their individual gifts and/or talents?

Were there opportunities for 'G&T' pupils to take on a mentoring role within the drama?

Did I create an opportunity within the drama work for pupils to continue their learning beyond the classroom and school day?

7

Measuring success

This chapter:

o describes the assessment processes used for drama as a model for other schools;
o proposes a model for progression from nursery to Year 6, covering artistic learning about drama and the social learning required by drama;
o outlines the 'Steps to Success in Drama' as an example of a local assessment framework which is benchmarked against national standards;
o describes the talk-related assessment for learning strategies used by learners and teachers in drama;
o considers how these, combined with choices about teaching style, bring to life the local steps to success and model of progression;
o offers a framework for evaluating the contribution that drama makes to a school improvement programme, by benchmarking evidence against nationally agreed standards of excellence.

Assessing social and artistic progress in drama

Rachel, a Year 5 class teacher reflects on her evaluations of her class at work in drama:

> When we first started drama, I found that I mostly evaluated from watching the children when they were working. When they are all on task, it is very interesting to watch the children interact with each other. It is fascinating to watch boys and girls mixing with each other without inhibitions as they are so focused on their work and enjoying each other's company. They also now value what others say, which wasn't always the case. The children seem to become their natural selves and they become very open with each other. It is wonderful just to hear some of the comments from the children when they don't think you are listening. They lose their hard images from the playground and their class position (which forms their identity within the classroom along with many of their actions) and simply enjoy each other.

Rachel's words are a reminder that the staff have great hopes for drama. Introducing drama was more to do with addressing a broad range of needs and concerns, as identified in Chapter 1, rather than with introducing an additional arts subject into an already crowded curriculum. This range stretched from concerns about pupils' lack of respect for each other (particularly in terms of gender, religious and ethnic differences) to a need for staff to rekindle and use their own creativity to make the curriculum more relevant and engaging for pupils.

From this perspective, the 'performance indicators' that Rachel identifies through informal observation, are focused on the social health of her class and the quality of their social learning through drama rather than on their progression in the dramatic skills of making, performing and responding. However, we argue that social learning and artistic learning are inter-related in drama – as we get better at one dimension of learning in drama so we also improve in the other. We also argue that children have an entitlement to an education in drama; they have a right to the support and information needed to get better at doing drama because it is an important subject in its own right as well as being central to a broader school improvement strategy. This means that children have an entitlement to a formal framework of assessment in drama in addition to the informal 'assessments' through observation that Rachel makes.

For these reasons, staff have developed a model of progression in both the social and artistic skills of drama. This model identifies key social and artistic skills to be developed in each year in the three strands of making, performing and responding to drama.

In order for the progression model to be used actively, as a guide to assessment-led teaching in drama (see Table 7.1), staff agreed these five principles for ensuring that teaching was geared to individual and class progression:

1 Pupils should be provided with a range of opportunities to demonstrate their abilities in different ways, and through different situations, across the key stages.
2 Assessment should be promoted as a form of personalised learning, used to raise self-esteem and motivate pupils through the teaching and learning.
3 Pupils should be actively involved in their own learning; opportunities and strategies should be created for pupils to assess themselves and each other in order to understand how they can build on and improve their own practice.
4 Activities should be created to address 'gaps' in pupils' understanding.
5 Planning should include selecting from a range of teaching styles to differentiate and personalise learning, and to enhance progression.

The model is used to make a diagnosis of how the class, as a unit of social learning, is progressing both artistically and socially. This class-level assessment forms the basis for discussion with pupils, and informs the talk-related

Table 7.1 A model of progression for assessment-led teaching in drama

Year End	Learning	Performance Indicators	Making	Performing	Responding
1	Social	*All*			
		Most	o Listen to and follow simple instructions.	o Take turns in the group work.	o Watch others' work.
		Some	o Respond to a given stimulus.		
	Artistic	*All*			
		Most	o Experiment with the dramatic skills and conventions used within the drama.	o Experiment with range of own voices, ie pace/pitch/tone.	o Comment on the drama work in performance.
		Some	o Identify how the drama develops from a given stimulus.	o Experiment with movement and gesture as a means of communication.	
2	Social	*All*			
		Most	o Listen to others in the group.	o Respond positively to others in the group.	o Watch others' work attentively.
		Some	o Form an opinion.		
	Artistic	*All*			
		Most	o Recognise and apply some dramatic skills and conventions used within the drama.	o Experiment with voice of their own accord.	o Appreciate the drama work in performance.
		Some	o Beginning to recognise that drama has a structure.	o Link movement with gesture in order to communicate meaning.	

3	Social	*All* *Most* *Some*	o Listen and focus on the ideas of others. o Voice own ideas.	o Contribute positively to the development of group work.	o Comment positively about other people's work. o Take an active role in evaluating own and others' work.
	Artistic	*All* *Most* *Some*	o Draw upon a number of dramatic skills and conventions in order to explore the drama. o Recognise how to structure the drama.	o Use voice to affect dramatic action. o Move with confidence and purpose.	
4	Social	*All* *Most* *Some*	o Listen and respond positively to the ideas of others. o Voice own ideas with confidence.	o Seek compromise rather than conflict. o Negotiate.	o Comment constructively about own and others' work.
	Artistic	*All* *Most* *Some*	o Identify and apply a number of dramatic skills and conventions to help explore the drama.	o Use the range and flexibility of own voice. o Understand how character is achieved through appropriate posture and gesture.	o Select from a critical vocabulary which can be applied to own work and that of others.
5	Social	*All* *Most* *Some*	o Structure the drama clearly. o Value the ideas of others when structuring the drama. o Realise own ideas in the development and structuring of the work.	o Recognise and respond appropriately to positive/negative behaviour within the group. o Negotiate with some effect.	o Edit and develop own work in light of constructive criticism.

(continued)

Table 7.1 Continued

Year End	Learning	Performance Indicators	Making	Performing	Responding
	Artistic	*All* *Most* *Some*	o Use a range of dramatic skills/conventions in order to explore and shape the drama. o Structure the drama with purpose and meaning.	o Use voice with energy and conviction. o Use movement and stillness to communicate dramatically within the space.	o Recognise some of the strengths and weakness of own and others' work in relation to the given task.
6	Social	*All* *Most* *Some*	o Recognise the importance of communication to develop the work. o Use own voice to shape and guide the direction of the work.	o Recognise and value the need for teamwork in order to respond effectively to the task. o Negotiate effectively.	o Edit and develop own work in light of constructive criticism.
	Artistic	*All* *Most* *Some*	o Select from appropriate dramatic skills/conventions in order to explore and shape the drama. o Structure the drama in order to communicate meaning.	o Draw upon a range of voices with energy and conviction. o Use body language/gesture and movement in order to sustain and develop dramatic action.	o Evaluate others' performances with an understanding of style and purpose.

assessment activities outlined later in this chapter. The end-of-year assessment of a class, together with individual assessments and levels of achievement make up a 'portfolio' to guide progression in the following year.

It is part of the Shenton Drama Policy that drama should be given equal status with National Curriculum core and foundation subjects. This means that individual children receive summative and formative assessments of their progress in drama, just as they do for other subjects (see Figure 7.1).

Name: Marium Begum				Year 4HG – Autumn Term	
What have we been working on in drama this term?					
Making	Always = ☺ Sometimes = 😐 Rarely = ☹	**Performing**	Always = ☺ Sometimes = 😐 Rarely = ☹	**Responding**	Always = ☺ Sometimes = 😐 Rarely = ☹
'I can...'		'I can...'		'I can...'	
Listen to people's ideas	☺	Show how a character feels through my voice	😐	Watch other peoples work	😐
Share my ideas with others	☺	I can stay 'in-role'	☹	Talk positively about other people's work	😐
Use still image and thought-tracking in my drama work	😐	Show how a character feels and thinks through body language	😐	Recognise good drama work	☺
My ➤◎ for NEXT term is to:		Stay 'in-role' when I am performing			End of term Level:
My teacher's ➤◎ for me NEXT term is to:		Think about how you can change your voice to match the character you are playing			**2**

Figure 7.1   Individual success in drama record

Table 7.2 Steps to success in drama

Pupils can: Level 5

Identify the dramatic potential of a wide range of stimuli, identifying possible tension, subtext, plot and theme. Negotiate with others both in and out of role. Draw on a range of dramatic techniques, genres and styles to convey character, situation, atmosphere and intention. Control body language and movement to develop character, matching dialect and register to role and situation. Explore space and levels to reflect meaning and use theatrical effects to create mood and tension, demonstrating an awareness of audience and purpose. Select from a range of objects and other technical effects and use these to enhance their work. Evaluate own and others' work in relation to intention. Adapt, refine and rehearse own work to develop purpose and meaning.

Level 4 *(average expected attainment end of KS2)*

Identify possible plot and theme in a variety of stimuli. Receive and sometimes give direction. Show awareness of how some dramatic techniques, genres and styles can be used to convey character and situation differently. Select voice, body language and movement appropriate to their character and can sustain a role. Use space and levels to reinforce meaning and are conscious of the relationship between actor and audience. Work with a range of objects and understand how they enhance meaning. Reflect on the strengths of their own and others' work, and comment on the relationship between intention and effect.

Level 3

Identify possible plot and theme in a variety of stimuli. Receive and sometimes give direction. Show awareness of how some dramatic techniques, genres and styles can be used to convey character and situation differently. Select voice, body language and movement appropriate to character and can sustain a role. Use space and levels to reinforce meaning and are conscious of the relationship between actor and audience. Work with a range of objects and understand how they enhance meaning. Reflect on the strengths of own and others' work, and comment on the relationship between intention and effect.

Level 2   (average expected attainment end of KS1)

Explore responses to a given stimulus through teacher-directed activities. Behave responsibly in small or whole group situations. Understand how they can develop their ideas through basic dramatic techniques. Use movement, body language and voice to express a range of simple characteristics and feel able to work with others in role. Use space and levels to shape their ideas and have some awareness of actor and audience. Pay attention to objects and how these can be used to engage and sustain interest. Comment on differences between own and others' work and suggest targets for improving their own work.

Level 1

Respond to a given stimulus through teacher-led questioning. Listen to and follow simple instructions. Recognise and have the ability to use basic dramatic techniques. Use movement and body language to express simple characteristics and respond to others in role. Demonstrate awareness of themselves and others around them and are attentive to objects (including costume) and their purpose within the space. Describe what they think and feel about others' work.

The termly assessment record of individual progress in drama is made up of two elements. The record indicates individual progress against the key social and artistic indicators for the year and also gives a level judgement based on the Steps to Success in Drama (see Table 7.2, pp. 148–9). These steps, or levels, were negotiated by staff and the external drama consultant, based on a local interpretation of the Arts Council's Drama Levels, published in the second edition of *Drama in Schools*.

The staff felt that the Arts Council Levels needed some local interpretation to give them and their pupils ownership over the language used to describe achievement. Staff also felt that the Arts Council levels were tied to particular social and cultural groups and were not responsive enough either to the cultural and social profile of their school, or to the wide range of objectives they had for drama.

Another important consideration in designing the Steps to Success was the need to benchmark progress in drama against level descriptions in National Curriculum subjects and assessment guidance in the National Literacy Strategy and Primary Strategy. In keeping with the assessment frameworks in most other National Curriculum subjects including music and art, the decision was taken to frame single level descriptors that include making, performing and responding rather than multiple descriptions for each strand.

Talk-related assessment routines

In keeping with the principles for social learning established in the contracting process, assessment in drama is based in an ongoing dialogue between teacher and the class as a unit of social learning and with individual pupils. This dialogue includes making negotiated assessments of individual and class progress towards the key artistic and social learning indicators for the year group as well as any other objectives the particular class might be working towards – getting better at staying in role for instance.

The assessments that are made are done publicly through dialogue and involve both pupils and teacher making judgements. The dialogue always includes negotiation of targets for improvement in both social and artistic domains of the work as well as setting targets to be covered in other subjects – to look again at an aspect of literacy for example.

Below are some of the talk-related assessment routines which are used regularly to involve pupils in the assessment process. These routines also place important social demands on pupils, which are in keeping with the objectives of the school improvement strategy. Pupils need to be able to offer and receive feedback from each other; they need to trust each other and respect the opinions of partners who may be from a different gender or culture to themselves; they need to feel confident enough with each to give public assessments of each other's work.

Figure 7.2   Applause and action

Applause and action

One simple strategy to ensure that peer assessment is a regular part of the drama work is to ask individual pupils to offer a point of 'applause' and a point of 'action' whenever watching the work of others. This is done by the teacher raising the appropriate card and naming a pupil in the audience to respond to what they have just seen. This strategy also keeps the audience attentive and trains the pupils to look at how work has been made and performed.

The 'applause' prompt develops skills in assessing what has been successful in the work and the 'action' prompt develops pupils' critical capabilities in understanding how practice can be improved. The consistent use of this strategy helps pupils to learn how to talk positively and constructively about each other's work, using achievements as a focus for discussion as well as to learn how everyone can improve their work through peer support and suggestions which are designed to boost confidence and fulfil the potential of the work.

'Progress partners'

In order to strengthen pupils' ability to reflect on and evaluate each other's progress, pupils work with a 'progress partner'. This should be someone with whom they can discuss and share their own progress and achievements. Progress partners also work together to find ways of improving their skills at 'doing drama'. Many pupils in primary schools are already used to 'buddy' systems and work effectively within them, either supporting younger pupils at break and lunchtimes or in their own classrooms for reading exercises. Creating opportunities for pupils to break free from the 'constraints' of friendship groups can be an energising and even therapeutic experience.

In allocating 'progress partners' the teacher might want to bring together pupils who would not necessarily choose to work with each other. This is another way of breaking down boundaries of gender and culture which can prevent effective social learning within a class. The assessment focus of 'progress partners', together with the need to agree an outcome, ensure that the partners have a clear and immediate purpose and agenda for talking together.

The ground rules for working with a 'progress partner' need to be discussed and agreed as part of the contracting process. These pupils give examples of what they want from their 'progress partner' – someone who 'builds up your confidence and doesn't put you down', 'wants you to improve', 'will be kind but honest when they "talk" about your work', and 'will be understanding of things you find difficult' in drama.

'Progress partners' can be used in a variety of ways in drama, in the context of either a formative strategy for assessing progress from one activity to the next, or of a summative strategy which assesses progress at the end of a particular unit of work or term.

Figure 7.3 shows a record card used by 'progress partners' during Term 1 in Year 4. (Compare this with Figure 7.1 on p. 147.) Pupils worked together to evaluate each other's ability 'to understand and use still image with effect'. In order to keep the process focused and enjoyable, pupils base their discussion of each other's progress on the simple guide of *always*, *sometimes* and *rarely*. Smiley stamps are used to mark their achievements in the three areas: ability to stay in role, ability to use body language to show a range of characteristics and ability to consider the audience when presenting.

The assessment focus is decided by the teacher and should be related to particular learning objectives (no more than three). Although there will have been all kinds of learning taking place within the drama work, both artistic and social, it is important not to try and assess everything at once. As in the assessment of National Curriculum subjects, pupils need to be able to draw on and use a range of skills such as making, performing and responding to show what they can do. Therefore it is important to plan for activities whereby all pupils are given the opportunity to demonstrate their achievements in different ways and at different times during the year.

Ready, Steady, Go!

This strategy works simply by drawing on the traffic light sequence of:

o **Amber** – what the class should *keep on* doing;
o **Red** – what the class should *stop* doing (see Figure 7.4, p. 154);
o **Green** – what the class should *start* doing (see Figure 7.5, p. 154).

This sequence could be used at the beginning of any drama activity (to build on previous work), during the drama activity (to focus on a particular behaviour

Assessment Focus: Understanding and using 'still image' with effect.		Year 4/ Term 1
Always ☺ / **S**ometimes 😐 / **R**arely ☹		
Ability to:	Bavisha can:	Mohammed can:
❶ Stay in role	☹	😐
❷ Use body language to show a range of characteristics	😐	😐
❸ Consider the audience when presenting	☺	☺
Bavisha's ➤—◎	Don't laugh when working 'in-role'	
Mohammed's ➤—◎	Match body language to character	

Figure 7.3   Assessment record card

pattern) or at the end (to evaluate how to progress in the next drama lesson). Unless there have been particular problems that are serious enough to begin with Red and Green lights, the teacher normally begins with Amber and a discussion of the positive features of the work which need to be maintained and encouraged.

Coloured cards signalling the 'keep doing' and 'stop'/'start' signs can be targeted at individuals or groups at any stage of the drama work. For instance, the teacher holds up the green card: 'Zara, I want you to START contributing some of your own ideas during the planning of your groups' work.' Or teacher holds up the red card and *then* the green card: 'Yassin, I want you to STOP blocking the

---

Whole class reminders!

What are you going to STOP doing?

For example:

○ talking over people when planning;

○ thinking that 'you' know best;

○ turning your back to the audience.

Figure 7.4   'STOP!'

Whole class reminders!

What are you going to START doing?

For example:

○ listening to other people's points of view;

○ thinking about how you could use facial expressions for different emotions;

○ being more aware of your audience when performing.

Figure 7.5   'START!'

girls out of the group and START to share your ideas with the whole group.'
Or the teacher holds up the amber card: 'Jack, I want you to KEEP on giving
direction to others in your group.'

This strategy is useful not only for monitoring and setting actionable targets for
individual progression, but also for indicating to *all* pupils that you recognise and
value what they *are* doing during the drama.

By acknowledging individual and class strengths and achievements, the teacher
uses assessment to motivate and reward while at the same time offering specific
guidance for 'acting' on those areas which are currently blocking progress. As
pupils become comfortable with this strategy they should be able to comment on
what they think they should start/stop/keep on doing in order to progress in
drama. By doing this they are taking responsibility for their own progress and
reflecting on the class's effectiveness as a unit of social learning.

Measuring up to excellence: benchmarking progress

The previous section of this chapter has outlined the assessment processes
and model of progression used to monitor pupil achievements in drama. This
section considers the assessment and evaluation of the 'holistic model' of drama

introduced and the extent to which drama has contributed to the broader aims of the programme. This evaluation serves as the conclusion to this book. Here Maggie, the headteacher, summarises the thinking behind the adoption of drama as a school improvement process in her school:

> The approach has been to adopt a holistic model of drama teaching and learning that has sought to include key personal and social objectives for the work, with developing dramatic skills and knowledge and through this learning to also develop pupils' competence as effective communicators.
>
> There is a further dimension to the drama project which is to do with drama's role in making the school a healthier community for all and more effective in terms of raising the standards of achievement and the aspirations of urban and culturally diverse children. Obviously the school needed some way of mapping and assessing progress across such a broad range of personal, social and academic objectives. In our view to focus on a narrow assessment of some aspects of drama, like literacy, might mean that progress in other directions went unnoticed. As it happens introducing drama has not, so far, proved to be a miraculous way of raising national test scores, but it has, we think made us all more effective and human teachers and learners.

Maggie reminds us that drama was introduced as part of a programme for improving the quality of life and learning in her primary school. It was not about 'bolting on' another subject, nor about a limited focus on using drama techniques to improve standards in individual subjects. At the core of the programme was a school-wide focus on pedagogy – how best we can teach and learn in this community. This focus on pedagogy could only be realised through bringing about changes in the culture of the school. These cultural changes included building a more positive, equitable and locally responsive climate for learning; developing collegiality among staff and social responsibility among pupils; reviewing and renewing models of curriculum and assessment so that they reflected the pupils' social, spiritual and cultural needs as well as the academic requirements set by the National Curriculum and National Literacy Strategy.

Despite the intensely local focus of the programme, concerned as it was with ways in which staff, pupils and the wider community of this particular school could harness and maximise their particular strengths and cultural backgrounds, the school still wanted to be sure that the improvement programme was producing evidence that could be benchmarked against appropriate external indicators applied by OfSTED and other agencies. In this way the claims made for drama could be evidence based against externally agreed standards of excellence.

In Chapter 2 we drew attention to two OfSTED reports which had a significant effect in shaping the pedagogical dimension of the school improvement programme: *Excellence and Enjoyment* and *The Curriculum in Successful Primary Schools*. During the programme, OfSTED produced additional reports which were useful as confirmation that the school was moving in the right directions; these included: *Expecting the Unexpected – Developing Creativity in Primary and Secondary Schools* and *Improving City Schools – How the Arts Can Help*. There has been increasing interest in creativity as a result of the publication of *All Our Futures – Creativity, Culture and Education* by the DfES and the National Advisory Committee on Creative and Cultural Education (NAACE). The DfES has also launched an advisory website *Creativity: Find it, Promote it* (www.ncaction.org.uk/creativity) which gives useful indicators of what creative teaching and learning looks like in a broad range of schools.

In 2003, the National College of School Leadership (NCLS) worked with a group of headteachers from successful schools. Drawing upon their experiences and expertise, together with an analysis of features of best practice drawn from the reports mentioned above, the College proposed an evaluatory framework for schools to use to assess their progress towards establishing a 'culture of creativity'.

Like Maggie, the headteacher at Shenton, these heads from leading edge schools agreed that there is more to a culture of creativity than a token insertion of creative techniques into an unreformed curriculum. They also agreed that a focus on pedagogy was central to creating a culture of creativity:

> Creative learning is much more than an allocation of more time for humanities and the arts. At the heart of these successful schools lies a culture of creativity that can best be described by a combination of relationships, organisation, teaching and learning (from *Primary Creativity and Curriculum*, NCSL 2003).

Performance indicators proposed by NCSL

The NCSL group proposed a number of sets of performance indicators, as laid out in Table A.2. We have provided evidence from Shenton's drama programme to match each of these indicators and provide evidence of the staff and pupils achievements working together to create the 'culture of creativity' which is now widely recognised as essential to the modernisation of primary schooling.

The gathering of evidence and the matching of evidence to the NCSL criteria was guided by the following question:

> What material evidence is there that our whole school focus on drama is moving us closer to matching external indicators of a 'creative culture'?

We hope that this evidence will also be useful for advocating drama to governors, parents and other teachers. The framework may also be useful as an evaluation strategy for your school once drama becomes established. Of course, drama is not the only contributing factor here. But the shared focus on rising to the 'big challenge' of drama has been central to a broad range of school improvement initiatives across the spectrum of learning and living experiences offered in the school. We present this benchmarking here as evidence that in an ordinary school like Shenton, an ordinary school like yours, drama really can make a substantial contribution to a positive, enabling and creative educational experience for pupils and teachers alike.

The NCSL performance indicators are outlined in Tables A.1, A.2 and A.3 in the Appendix to this book.

Looking ahead

The staff at Shenton Primary School continue their journey towards improving the quality of learning and of living in their school. Some of them have moved on, taking their skills with them and beginning again in another school. New teachers arrive, and are given support as they discover the uses of drama within the school. Our story ends here, but theirs – like yours – continues. Whether you read and use this book as a learning community, or whether you read it as a lone but determined voice in your school, we wish you well and hope that we have given you tools that will help you put the case for drama as a wide ranging and effective school improvement strategy.

Appendix

NCSL performance indicators

Table A.1   Attitudes, behaviours and relationships

Performance Indicator	Evidence of attainment
The schools are warm and welcoming	○ Pupils are more confident and open to visitors ○ The drama contract has helped pupils to feel safe in their learning ○ Displays of drama-related work and photographs have brought colour and life to corridors and entrance
There is a sense of community	○ Parents and community leaders join in assemblies, performances, workshops and drama clubs ○ Pupils are more supportive of each other and recognise their social responsibllity as community members ○ The contracting process has provided a focus for teacher–pupil discussions about behaving and learning together
The schools are inclusive	○ Drama has successfully accelerated social learning in mixed ability settings for all pupils including those with EAL, SEN and G&T ○ Drama requires teachers and pupils to use prior knowledge and cultural experiences in the classroom ○ Pupils' work in drama has increased empathy and tolerance of 'difference'

A shared vision gives the school a strong sense of purpose and direction	o The holistic focus on school improvement through drama has given all staff a clear sense of direction o Teachers feel a real sense of ownership: the drama initiative is in their control o Teachers feel that their professional skills are valued and useful
Respect and trust extend across the whole school community	o Pupil relationships have improved in classroom and playground o Pupils feel that their prior knowledge and home cultures are getting more respect from teachers in drama o The drama initiative has involved staff in openly taking risks together and the collegial approach has increased professional respect among teachers and others
Members of staff are willing to support one another	o All drama planning and teaching has been collaborative between pairs of teachers, year teams, Key Stage teams and whole staff meetings o Teachers have felt confident enough to discuss problems and concerns as well as successes o Working together in drama has strengthened bonds between teachers and LSAs
Pupils show enjoyment, excitement and enthusiasm for school	o Pupils enjoy drama and look forward to it o Pupils refer to their drama work in other subjects o Parents report that pupils talk enthusiastically about their drama work at home
Challenge is evident throughout the school	o Teacher and pupils alike are conscious they have risen to the 'big challenge' of drama o Teachers and pupils are proud of the progress they have made in drama o Teachers are more willing and likely to take informed risks in other areas of teaching and learning

(continued)

Table A.1   Continued

Performance Indicator	Evidence of attainment
Pupils are keen to explore and display high levels of interest	o Drama has proved to be a motivational method of teaching which engages pupils at a feeling level and arouses their curiosities about the world o Drama has provided a means of social learning which is exploratory, creative and open-ended in terms of outcomes o Teachers have enjoyed 'exploring' stories and situations with their pupils in drama and learning from the pupils' contributions and ideas
They have high levels of confidence and self-esteem	o Acting and performing in front of others has increased confidence and improved communication and self-presentation skills o The emphasis on 'self-realisation' through active involvement in drama has increased the self-esteem of pupils o Teachers and pupils validate each other and have a clearer sense of their strengths and what they contribute to the team
Pupils' opinions are valued and their needs are recognised	o The focus on differentiation and behaviour management in drama has helped pupils to feel that their cultural, emotional and personal needs are considered in planning and teaching o The contract has provided frequent dialogue about the needs of both pupils and teachers o Pupils' ideas and opinions are used to develop the drama, and are an important focus of the reflection on what has been learnt in the drama
Pupils enjoy peer support or 'buddies'	o Intercultural and gender relationships have improved through the social demands of working together in drama o The 'buddy' system of peer assessment has helped pupils to be constructive and positive in giving feedback on each other's performance o Learning to work positively together in the social learning context of drama has affected group and class work across the curriculum

Table A.2   Features of organisation

Performance Indicator	Evidence of attainment
Imaginative use of budgets	○ Budgets have been used creatively to fund external consultant, theatre visits and artist workshops ○ Neighbourhood Renewal, Urban Regeneration and other sources of social funding have been used to support parent drama groups ○ School's initiative now recognised through Creative Partnership funding from Arts Council England
Creative solutions to problems	○ Drama has been used holistically to address a range of social, personal and professional issues in the academic and pastoral curricula ○ Specific problems in literacy, such as under-achievement in writing are addressed through drama work
Creative use and organisation of time	○ Drama has proved to be an effective means of combining subject learning, arts education and personal and social learning in one lesson or scheme of work ○ Improvements in behaviour and pupil relationships means more time on task across the curriculum ○ Establishing drama as a curriculum entitlement for all pupils means they have regular access to creative and artistic opportunities
Whole days or longer blocks of time for special projects	○ By combining subject learning with drama, longer periods of time can be released for sustained work in drama ○ Arts days are now a regular feature on the calendar ○ Special drama projects organised to honour festivals, times of the year and significant events such as Refugee Week or Remembrance Day

(continued)

Table A.2   Continued

Performance Indicator	Evidence of attainment
Work based on themes that make links between subjects	○ All schemes of work make reference to drama ○ Story dramas have provided a common context for cross-curricular work ○ Drama has linked academic learning with social and personal learning
Imaginative ways of grouping pupils together	○ Arts days organised for year groups to work together ○ Drama requires a variety of groupings from pairs to whole class; breaks down peer, cultural and gender boundaries ○ Drama has taught pupils to work as teams with shared responsibility for setting and achieving targets
Creative use of staffing to secure the best possible adult : child ratio	○ Drama co-ordinator released to work alongside NQTs ○ LSAs actively involved in teaching the drama – by taking roles for instance
Using the school environment to reflect the commitment to creative learning	○ There is a dedicated drama space with displays, images of pupils at work and drama-specific language and events ○ Displays of classroom work enhanced by drawing, writing and other visual and creative work produced in drama ○ Displays of story-based drama work encourage pupils of different ages to share the stories and drama experiences they have had

Table A.3   Features of teaching and learning

Performance Indicator	Evidence of attainment
An emphasis, wherever possible, on problem-solving and an enquiry-based approach to learning	o Confidence in drama means that pupils and teachers regularly work in a problem-solving and inquiry-based method of teaching and learning o The focus on story and role play allows pupils to ask questions about human behaviour; why people behave as they do in different situations o Drama also provides a context for an enquiry-based approach to resolving actual problems in the teaching group such as intolerance and a lack of respect for others
Willingness to take risks	o The positive 'can do' climate in drama has encouraged children to find their voices and use them without fear of censure or ridicule o Teachers are supported and encouraged at every level to take informed risks and have more confidence in this as a result of their successes in drama o Pupils are more willing to take risks in terms of cross-gender and cross-cultural learning and working together; they are more open to influences beyond their home and faith cultures
A culture of professional support that extends throughout the school	o Key Stage managers are willing to model good practice in drama for colleagues o Sharing good practice and ideas for drama is a regular item at staff meetings o Drama co-ordinator monitors planning and observes lessons to support colleagues

(continued)

Table A.3   Continued

Performance Indicator	Evidence of attainment
The celebration of innovation and imagination in teaching and learning	o Working in role has increased imaginative and creative skills for teachers and pupils o Teachers and pupils have learnt to be more flexible, innovative and creative in their teaching and learning o Teachers and pupils share a sense of achievement in terms of the obvious progress made in drama
The encouragement of collaboration between pupils and between teachers	o Increased confidence and skill in using questioning and learning through discovery allows teachers to give greater responsibility to pupils for the direction of their learning o The contracting process ensures ongoing dialogue between teachers and pupils and negotiated targets and goals for the drama work o Teachers regularly plan, discuss and debrief their drama work together
Recognition of the need to take account of preferred learning styles	o Working in drama has made teachers more aware of their pupils' preferred learning styles o Drama highlights visual and kinaesthetic learning styles and uses multimodal forms of communication o Drama has helped pupils to link cognitive and affective learning, subject and personal and social learning

Opportunities for pupils to work independently and collaboratively, and to learn collectively	○ Drama work has developed the quality and outcomes of social learning across the curriculum ○ Drama has trained pupils to be more open and positive about working across genders and cultures ○ Innovative and performance-related peer and self-assessment processes introduced through drama
Time for pupils to persevere with extended pieces of work	○ Drama has provided opportunities for follow-up work in the classroom and enrichment tasks ○ G&T pupils do additional research and drama-related tasks out of school and are given extra-curricular drama time ○ 'Mantle of the Expert' projects give extended periods of time on cross-curricular practical 'real-world' tasks
Use of the knowledge and skills of visitors, and members of the wider community	○ External consultants, local theatres, artists and MA students have all been actively involved in the school improvement programme ○ Mulannas and other community leaders have been actively involved in shaping and supporting the drama programme ○ Because parents have discussed drama with their children and been involved in workshops they feel involved in the aims and objectives of the programme
Enrichment of learning, wherever possible, by first-hand experience within and beyond the school	○ Learning through the imagined 'first hand' experience of drama has made learning more concrete and accessible for EAL, SEN and those pupils with restricted social and cultural experiences

References

Arts Council of England (2003) *Drama in Schools*, 2nd edition. London: Arts Council of England.

DfES (2003) *The National Literacy Strategy*. London: DfES.

DfES (2003) *The Primary National Strategy: speaking, listening, learning*. London: DfES.

NAACE (2004) *All Our Futures – Creativity, Culture and Education*. London: DfES.

National Council of School Leaders (2003) *Primary Creativity and Curriculum*. London: NCSL.

Neelands, J. and Goode, T. (2000) *Structuring Drama Work*. Cambridge: Cambridge University Press.

OfSTED (2002) *The Curriculum in Successful Primary Schools*. London: OfSTED. www.ofsted.gov.uk

OfSTED (2003) *Excellence and Enjoyment – A Strategy for Primary Schools*. London: OfSTED. www.standards.dfes.gov.uk

Books for children on which schemes of work are modelled in the text

McKee, D. (2005) *The Conquerors*. London: Andersen Press.

McKee, D. (2005) *Not now Bernard*. London: Andersen Press.

A full list of references and resources used, including all the books for children mentioned in this book, is given on the publisher's website – www.fultonpublishers.co.uk

Index

active learners 76
alternate roles 129
alternative scenes 64
anthropologists 12
anti-social behaviour 11
applause 149–51
art 87
Arts Council England (ACE) 21, 26, 27 150, 161
assessment 142–54
aural learners 75, 77, 119
Aztecs example 94–5

behaviour 47–8; anti-social behaviour 11; challenging behaviour 126
behaviour checklist 50–1
behaviour contracts 40
benchmarking 154–64
body language 49, 148
budgets 161
bullying 14, 120

challenging behaviour 126
characters 66
circles 42–3
classroom management 48–50
The Conquerors, David McKee 24, 106, 133–40
conventions 105–8, 109–16
conversations 65, 81, 93, 106, 121, 122, 137–8
'Creative Generation' website (GTEU) 27–8

D&T 86
DfES 20, 155
diary writing 74, 114–15, 132
differentiation 140–1, 160
dilemmas 73–4
drama co-ordinators 7, 8, 163
Drama in Schools, ACE 21–2, 25, 27, 150

EAL (English as an additional language) pupils 1, 70, 71, 117, 120–5, 132–7, 139, 140, 158, 165; integration 120–1; work/talk partners 121
end-of-year assessment 147
English (subject) 18, 20, 86
environments 68–9, 77, 108; non-judgemental environments 127–8
eye contact 49

finger puppets 81
flashbacks 44

G&T (gifted and talented) pupils 2, 117, 129–32, 133, 135–9, 140, 141, 158, 165
gender-specific difficulties 41
geography 87
gestures 64, 111, 112, 129
Gifted & Talented Education Unit (GTEU) 27
ground rules 38–41
group work 45–6, 122

headlines 84
history 59, 86
hot seating 63

ICT 89
images 71, 124
inclusion 117–41, 158; differentiation 140–1; EAL pupils 117, 120–5, 132, 133, 134, 136, 137, 139, 140; G&T pupils 117, 129–32, 133, 135–41; SEN pupils 117, 125–9, 132, 133, 135–40
inner speech 64
integration: EAL pupils 120–1

Key-Stage-1 18–19, 22–3, 40, 90, 93; group work 45–6, 102–3; statutory requirements 19; *Three Strands* framework 25
Key-Stage-2 18–19, 22–3, 40, 45, 90, 93–4, 103, 132–40; group work 45–6; statutory

requirements 19; *Three Strands* framework 25, 26
Key-Stage-3 21, 28
Key-Stage-4 21
kinaesthetic learners 71, 77
kinaesthetic learning 119, 164
King Lear 108, 109–16

lighting 124
Little Red Riding Hood (LRRH) 63–5
LSAs (learning support assistants) 5, 31, 159, 162

management strategies 6; classroom management 48–50
Mantle of the Expert 101–5, 107, 165
mathematics 89, 129–30
mime 129, 166
missing scenes 64
music 87

National Advisory Committee on Creative and Cultural Education (NAACE) 155
National College of School Leadership 156–65
National Curriculum 6, 11, 18, 30, 147, 155; English (subject) 18, 20; Key Stage 1 18–19, 25; Key Stage 2 18–19, 25–6; Key Stage 3 21, 28; Key Stage 4 21; statutory requirements 19
National Literacy Strategy 6, 17, 18, 20–1, 28, 150, 155
National Numeracy Strategy 6
National Primary Strategy 17, 18, 28, 43–4, 150
Nightingale, Florence 59, 69
Noah's Ark 78–90, 105, 107
non-judgemental environments 127–8
Not Now Bernard, David McKee 52–6, 106, 107
nursery children 90, 92, 102

OfSTED 29, 32, 155
Oi, Get Off My Train, John Burningham 24

PE 88
performance indicators 143
physical theatre 26
plots 66
Primary National Strategy 17, 18, 28, 43–4, 144
progress partners 151–2
props 69, 77
puppets 21, 43–4

RE 88
recurring themes 66

rehearsing 12, 20, 46, 76, 119, 122
ritual 128–9
role play 13, 48, 58, 68
roles 55, 63, 68, 94, 126, 129, 133, 140, 162

science 59, 86
sculpting 54–5
Seacole, Mary 59
SEN (special educational needs) pupils 2, 117, 125–9, 132, 133, 135–6, 138–40, 158, 165
settings 66
Shenton Primary School 1–11, 16, 25–6, 29, 35, 104, 144, 156, 157, 162; *Tudors at sea* example 4–5
Sleeping Beauty 70–8, 108
sound 75
sound effects 124
spatial awareness 76
status 17, 99, 124, 147
statutory requirements (National Curriculum) 19
stories 58–90; characters 66; *Little Red Riding Hood* 63–5; *Noah's Ark* 78–90, 105, 107; plots 66; settings 66; *Sleeping Beauty* 70–8, 108; themes 62, 66, 67
story boxes 67–9
story games 65
Structuring Drama Work, Jonathan Neelands & Tony Goode 108–9
subtext 63
symbols 129, 140

Teacher-in-role 94–101, 114, 119–20, 166
tension 178
themes 62, 67, 113, 162; recurring themes 66
think-pair-share 44
thought-showers 70
thought-tracking 106, 138
Three Strands framework 25–6
topic boxes 68
topics 103–5
traffic light sequence 152–4
transitions 128
Tudors at sea example 4–5

visual learners 71, 77
visual learning 119, 164
visual symbols 129

W questions 97
word banks 125
word tennis 44
work/talk partners 121